MW01532393

ENDURING
URGENCY

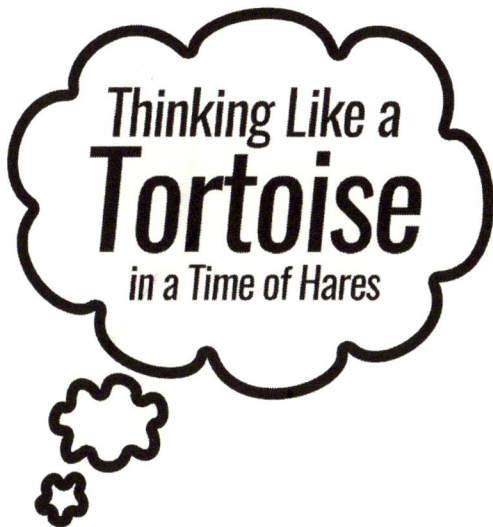

Thinking Like a
Tortoise
in a Time of Hares

DAVID A. BROWN-DAWSON

ENDURING URGENCY

PEOPLE WE MEET MEDIA

Enduring Urgency: Thinking Like a Tortoise in a Time of Hares
Copyright © 2020 by David Brown-Dawson

ISBN# 978-1-7346037-0-5

Any Internet addresses (websites, blogs, etc.), telephone numbers, and social media handles in this book are offered as a resource. They are not intended in any way to be or imply an endorsement by People We Meet Media, nor does People We Meet Media vouch for the content of these sites, numbers, and handles for the life of this book.

All rights reserved. No part of this book may be reproduced, stored in a retrieval system, or transmitted in any form or by any means – electronic, mechanical, photocopy, recording, or any other – except for brief quotations in printed reviews, without prior permission from the publisher.

Requests for information or permission should be addressed to:
People We Meet Media, LLC
P.O. Box 8802
Emeryville, CA 94662

Or

Enduringurgency@gmail.com

Anne-Marie!
Thank you for supporting this project. Without a doubt you are a very resilient person. I admire the way you approach studying for and taking the bar and the courage it took to share your journey. I hope you find value in the pages that follow.

To my family, thank you for your love and support all my life. I love each of you more than I can express. Thank you for loving me for me.

This book is dedicated to you who are reading these words. My hope is that something within this book strikes a chord with you, exposes you to a new idea, encourages you to grow, and helps you pursue your purpose effectively over time.

The world needs YOU and all of your gifts.

Much love,
David A. Brown-Dawson
13 May 2020

ENDURING URGENCY

CONTENTS

ENDURING URGENCY AND WHY WE NEED IT

There is important work to be done. Today. Children need to be raised, cures need to be developed, people need to be educated, homes need to be built, code needs to be written, songs need to be sung, clean water needs to be provided, scripts need to be produced. We may not be able to fix all the issues today, but that does not excuse us from doing good when we can where we are with what we have. People are hurting and using distractions to cope; people are stuck in complacency when they could be living a fuller life; people are allowing themselves to be divided instead of embracing each other; people are not living in their purpose, and they are leaving problems unsolved that they were created to solve.

The Enduring Urgency strategy is not some feel-good sentiment or mediocre motivation that you apply for the first month of the year when you are energized about your goal and the last two months of the year when you realize how far from accomplishing your goal you are. It is the mindset that enables you to work consistently each month, each week, each day so you arrive at your goals early and focused. The Enduring Urgency strategy is having an accurate understanding of yourself and unrelenting persistence towards your goals despite the adversity that may come your way and the time that may be required.

The West Wing, produced from 1999 to 2006, is a television show about the West Wing of the White House and the work that the president's staff does. In it, one of the characters, Josh, is going through a tough time battling depression and post-traumatic stress after being shot. Josh's boss and the president's Chief of Staff, Leo, has experienced tough times as an alcoholic and divorcee. In this specific episode, Josh is trying to hide his struggle but other people on his team can see it. Josh sits down with a trauma therapist at Leo's insistence and begins to make progress. Josh finishes his first session and to his surprise Leo is waiting for him with the following story:

This guy is walking down the street when he falls in a hole. The walls are so steep he can't get out. A doctor passes by and the guy shouts up, "Hey you, can you help me out?" The doctor writes a prescription, throws it down in the hole, and moves on. Then a priest comes along, and the guy shouts up, "Father, I am down in this hole. Can you help me out?" The priest writes out a prayer, throws it down in the hole, and moves on. Then a friend walks by. "Hey Joe, it's me. Can you help me out?" And the friend jumps in the hole. Our guy says, "Are you stupid? Now we're both down here." The friend says, "Yeah, but I've been down here before and I know the way out."

Leo goes on to tell Josh that he is there for him and that as long as Leo has a job, Josh has a job.[1]

There are times when we choose to be tough and in doing so eliminate the opportunity for someone to help us. I don't like people thinking I am weak and I hate being a burden on people. That said, through my experiences, I have realized people are willing to help if you are humble enough to ask. Moreover, in sharing your pain or your limitations, you empower others to share their own. Authentic relationships are built when we have genuine conversations. When you understand you are not the only person dealing with a problem, it is encouraging. Many times, there are people who have dealt with a similar situation before who are willing to help you through it.

If you feel trapped in a hole, please imagine this book as me jumping down in the hole with you. If you know someone who feels trapped in a hole, consider gifting this book to them as a metaphor of you jumping in to help them.

If you are not struggling in life, but you want to improve, be better, and do better, this book is also for you. Sometimes when we reach our goals, we get complacent. It's one thing to get there. It's another thing to be consistent, stay there, and continue to improve.

I won't pretend to understand specifically what you are going through. But I have been through enough to understand how resilience, patience, and consistent focused action are crucial to effectiveness, impact, and achieving your goals.

I feel an urgency as I am writing this. Because if me sharing my heart, my life lessons, and the tools I've used can help get you out of the hole, can help you become whole, or can elevate you to your next level of life, I want that for you. And I want that for you today. It is time to adopt a new approach to life. It is time to live life with Enduring Urgency.

Instead of focusing on the larger issues, I am taking a more focused approach. From my life experiences, books I have read, and people I have met, I wanted to share my syncretized approach to life. It is, as you have surmised, the title of this book: *Enduring Urgency.*

We need Enduring Urgency. I will unpack this idea throughout the course of this book. I am an engineer by nature and by degree, so I would like to present you with the equation that underpins this book:

$$\textit{Enduring Urgency} =$$
$$\textit{Resilience + Patience + Consistent Focused Action}$$

Patience and consistent focused action are required to build resilience. Consistent focused action and resilience are required to develop patience. And resilience and patience are required to take consistent focused action.

Why am I writing this now, and what enables me to speak on this idea?

Simply put, I am writing this now because it needs to be written now. I am writing this book out of love for you reading it. Love is needed now. Awareness is needed now. Empathy is needed now. Compassion is needed now. Unity is needed now. Enduring Urgency is needed now.

As far as I can, I am living this right now. I thought about waiting until I had reached a measure of success before writing this book, but I was using my current age and stage of life as an excuse to delay. The people I have met, my life experiences, and this strategy have all brought me to this point in time. I have a responsibility to articulate this strategy. I have gone through the rougher parts and I am still growing through this process. What makes it better is that you will see how I continue to operate with a spirit of Enduring Urgency as we continue down this road of life together.

I could have waited to write this book for another 25 years or when the world had deemed me "successful". There are two main reasons I did not want to do that: I would have missed influencing and equipping an entire generation and it would have been against the message of this book.

The first time I explained the full concept of this book was in a conversation with one of my best friends, Jonathon.

The idea behind Enduring Urgency is that there is a lot of good work to be done NOW, and we cannot sit back and expect others to do it. There must be a desire to act now (Consistent Focused Action) together with an understanding that improvement takes time (Patience) and the ability to recover quickly from difficulties and setbacks (Resilience).

By itself, "Urgency" speaks to the need for focused action. A definition of urgency is *Importance requiring swift action*.[2] But what happens when these actions don't go your way? Or you experience adversity? How long will you need to stay focused? Operating solely in a state of urgency brings exhaustion over time.

"Enduring" on its own captures the qualities of resilience and patience when dealing with something difficult for an extended period. But it completely misses the concept of consistent focused action.

Bringing the two words together produces a complete concept and a useful strategy. There is a situation of importance requiring swift action (urgency); that important work may not be easy, and improvements may not happen immediately (the urgency needs to endure). Nevertheless, it is important to consistently act now.

I have been blessed to live in Texas, California, Washington D.C., New Jersey, and Japan. I have been able to travel throughout the United States of America, throughout Asia, and throughout Africa. It is fascinating how much we all have in common when we move past our presumed differences and take the chance to have real conversations. As I meet people, and get to know their stories, understanding occurs. In time, I go from being ignorant and indifferent to being aware, to being compassionate, empathetic, and ultimately being an advocate for those who are experiencing injustice and harsh realities.

LEGACY LENSES

I talked to my buddy Reggie while he was putting the finishing touches on his daughter's room in preparation for her arrival. We talked about how excited he was to be a father, how his wife was doing, how they were preparing for their baby girl's arrival, and what kind of life they want to provide her.

He talked about wanting to set a good example for her, so when she is older, she is a well-rounded, aware, thoughtful, and productive member of society. He understood that their actions and choices over the next few years would set their daughter up for either success or failure.

His final thought was, "We want to improve for her, but also for ourselves."

I believe Reggie is viewing life with legacy lenses. Seeing with legacy lenses is part of the Enduring Urgency strategy. This means understanding that there is work to do now but knowing and being okay with the fact that it will be a long-term process and you will face adversity.

The idea of Enduring Urgency can be captured by closing your eyes and imagining you are wearing glasses. Except with these lenses, you can see two generations from now in your family tree. What do you see? What do you want to see? What is the best-case scenario? Now, what will it take right now to bring about that best-case scenario?

The story of *Honi* the Circle Maker captures the idea of living with legacy lenses. One day, Honi was walking on the road and saw a man planting a carob tree. Honi asked the man, "How long will it take for this tree to bear fruit?"

The man replied, "Seventy years."

Honi then asked the man, "And do you think you will live another seventy years and eat the fruit of this tree?"

The man answered, "Perhaps not. However, when I was born into this world, I found many carob trees planted by my father and grandfather. Just as they planted trees for me, I am planting trees for my children and grandchildren, so they will be able to eat the fruit of these trees."[3]

Living with legacy lenses means seeing who we are and who we want to be, seeing who we want our children and grandchildren to be, what we want humanity to be, and doing whatever it takes in our lifetime to lay the necessary foundation.

We understand that we may not see the dream realized, but we are doing our part to further the dream. We plant the fruit tree and water it daily, knowing we may not be benefactor of its fruit.

Enduring Urgency is about doing what needs to be done today with an understanding that the impact and benefit may not be realized for years and possibly generations. Delayed gratification is part of operating with legacy lenses. Too often we fall prey to the microwave and instant gratification mindset of wanting to see the fruits of our labor right now. But that is not how the process works. It is consistently watering the seeds in your garden even when nothing is showing on the surface; it is consistently running even though you do not feel your endurance building; it is working at your craft while no one is watching so that you are ready to seize your opportunity regardless of who is watching.

Enduring Urgency is a mindset that can impact your individual life, your family, and your community for generations to come.

THE COST

There is a cost to operating with the Enduring Urgency mindset. I wish I could tell you that by implementing the Enduring Urgency strategy, you will no longer face adversity. But that's not reality. Other strategies can help you through the good days. This strategy is for every day, including the tough days. And there will be tough days, if there haven't been already. There will be days when you feel like giving up, days when you feel you aren't good enough, days when you are exhausted, days when you feel like crying. These are normal thoughts and feelings. It is how we handle the tough days that will define our success. Denzel Washington put it this way: "Ease is a greater threat to progress than hardship." Operating with Enduring Urgency can improve your situation and it is the strategy that keeps those on top, on top.

I am thrilled you are reading this book and I hope it encourages, equips, and challenges you. Before continuing, here are two requests and a dare.

1) Take the next minute to write down what you expect to get from this book.

2) Write out your personal definition of success.

Now, I DARE YOU to read this book cover-to-cover in the next seven days. Then, you can carry this book around and return to relevant sections whenever you need to.

NOTES

THINKING LIKE A TORTOISE IN A TIME OF HARES

A subtitle like this may seem odd and it may be what caught your attention. I've always liked the story of the tortoise and the hare. In writing this book, I researched different versions and watched videos about the story. In doing so it struck me that this story can be a metaphor for Enduring Urgency, and a warning against the opposite approach to life, complacent apathy.

The tortoise exhibited the factors that constitute Enduring Urgency: resilience, patience, and consistent focused action. Many interpretations have been written about this fable, ranging from deep proverbs to satirical commentaries. I will use the story to illustrate the characteristics of Enduring Urgency and to advocate for its implementation in your life. If the analogy of the tortoise and the hare doesn't match completely in your head, my hope is that the ideas surrounding Enduring Urgency will.

The pivotal distinction here is *"Thinking* Like a Tortoise in a Time of Hares". This tortoise versus hare competition is not external; it is internal. I am not in competition with anyone besides myself. As I learn and continue to master this tortoise mindset internally, I become more successful and people may see it externally. (We'll talk more about *success* later.)

A TIME OF HARES

Let's start with the hare: He was boastful. He antagonized the tortoise for the tortoise's abilities, or rather perceived inabilities. The hare was fast, which is not a bad thing in itself.

He did have abilities, but he did not fully understand his strengths and weaknesses, or he simply chose not to address them. He did not value nor take seriously the abilities of the tortoise, which led to him becoming complacent, opening the door for him to be distracted, and ultimately losing the race.

By themselves, speed and confidence are not bad traits. However, when combined with complacency, a lack of compassion, being disrespectful, focusing on the crowd, and being easily distracted, it is a recipe for disaster.

Many times, we are the hare, allowing ourselves to be distracted by social media, television, the negative aspects of our lives, or other peoples' lives. We think we have all the time in the world and we underestimate the hard work and dedication required to achieve our goals. We get complacent in our daily lives, and then we are upset when we see others achieving what we feel entitled to.

Other times, we allow our preconceived notions of someone or the information we come across to negatively shape our view of someone else without doing our due diligence. We allow what we see about someone on social media to define our view of their whole person, not accounting for the other dimensions of their personality and life. We think that because someone is different, they are inferior, incapable, or deserve to be mistreated.

We must not fall victim to the hare mentality. We must not allow ourselves to be distracted from the things that matter. We must know our true self; we must steward our abilities and account for our weaknesses; we must stay focused and run our own race; we must operate with an enduring sense of urgency.

Thinking Like a Tortoise

Now, let's focus to the tortoise. His name was "Slow and Steady" in Aesop's original fable. We do not get much background about Slow and Steady other than he was finally fed up with the boasting of the hare and he made up his mind to act. He knew himself enough to know that he was not faster than the hare, so he moved with a consistent sense of urgency, and he ran his own race.

Bonus conjecture: The tortoise had seen the hare enough to know what the hare's strengths and weaknesses were, and he hypothesized that the hare would get distracted. The tortoise had a keen awareness of what was occurring around him, without allowing it to distract him. The tortoise knew that regardless of the hare's abilities and actions, he must stay focused and keep moving forward to be victorious.

I chose the subtitle "Thinking Like a Tortoise" as opposed to "being" or "acting", because I do not believe everything must be done slowly. When I think of a tortoise, I think of longevity, patience, and toughness.

The Tortoise – Beyond the Race

The tortoise is the longest living land animal known in the world with most species of tortoise living between 80 and 150 years.

A tortoise has both an exoskeleton and an endoskeleton. The exoskeleton consists of the carapace (the shell) above its flesh and the plastron (the hard plate under the turtle) below. The endoskeleton consists of the spine, collar-bone, and ribs. The exoskeleton is connected to the endoskeleton. In other words, the shell is part of the tortoise. Though the shell is hard, the tortoise can still feel everything that touches it. When it is attacked, it can still feel the pressure and the pain of the attack. However, that pain is dulled by the shell similar to humans' finger nails. Because of the shell, the tortoise lives. The shell is for immediate and consistent protection. The tortoise's shell is its built-in resilience.

The Latin word for tortoise is *testudo*. The ancient Roman military would take up the testudo formation during a siege, which meant they could move forward deliberately while maintaining protection. That the Roman military used the strategy of a tortoise speaks to its effectiveness.

It is one level to have a spine, collar-bone, and ribs, as we humans do. But the tortoise's shell acts as a shield against predators, potential attacks, and the environment. As we build up our own resilience, we can withstand the adversity that occurs in life as we live in our purpose and pursue our goals.

When we discuss patience regarding Enduring Urgency, we are talking about an active patience. The patience of the tortoise in the fable was displayed by his willingness to keep moving consistently even while the hare slept. Patience is also revealed in the longevity of a tortoise, and its ability to endure life, attacks, and its environment often for over 120 years.

Consistent focused action is revealed in the way the tortoise started the race, moved throughout the race, and finished the race. The tortoise remained focused and did not allow the crowd, the environment, nor the hare to keep him from his goal.

Though times have changed since the days of the ancient Romans and since the time this fable was written, and technology has sped up many aspects of our world, there is great benefit in thinking like a tortoise – being resilient, practicing patience, and taking consistent focused action.

<u>NOTES</u>

SECTION I: RESILIENCE

Resilience: The capacity to recover quickly from difficulties; toughness. [4]

Resilience: A set of processes that enables good outcomes in spite of serious threats. The ability to persist in the face of challenges and to bounce back from adversity. [5]

Resilience (scientific definition): The capability of a strained body to recover its size and shape after deformation caused especially by compressive stress. [6]

In the summer of my 17th year, I was on vacation with my family in Puerto Vallarta. The night of our arrival, my sister, Anna, and I saw a large trampoline about 100 meters into the water from the shore of the hotel's beach and decided we would check it out the following day.

I have always enjoyed French toast and at breakfast the next morning, they did not disappoint. I indulged in two helpings of French toast among other delicious items and enjoyed every bite. With breakfast complete, my sister and I decided to explore the resort grounds to see what all was available. As we walked toward the beach, we again saw the yellow and blue water trampoline calling our name from the open water and we decided to answer. We told our parents our plan for the day, changed into our swimwear, and took off. It was a beautiful day as we started the swim out to the trampoline, the water was calm but wavy.

About a third of the way there, I started to feel the French toast shifting around my stomach. My sister was ahead of me – admittedly she was a stronger swimmer – so I pushed to keep up. Two-thirds of the way there, the first cramp hit me, and I let Anna know. We were closer to the trampoline than to the shore, so she encouraged me and said we would rest when we got to the trampoline before jumping. The final third of the swim consisted of me gulping down a few mouthfuls of salty seawater, which increased my cramps and added to my exhaustion. I resolved that I could make it to the trampoline, but in the back of my mind I was starting to panic.

We arrived at the trampoline exhausted but excited, but we could not find the handles to get up the trampoline. From the shore the trampoline looked large but traversable. Once we got closer, we realized the top was five feet out of the water, slick, and curved around the sides. Our horror grew as we swam its circumference and found the rubber handles and footsteps had broken off. That's when the full-on panic set in. I was physically exhausted, and Anna could see it in my face. She went into big sister-protector mode. We were on the far side of the trampoline-deathtrap at this point and I could no longer see land. I was able to find the rope that was anchoring the trampoline in place and grabbed onto it. Unfortunately, it was attached under the trampoline, so my head would submerge and pop back up every few seconds. This was unsustainable, and we knew we had to move. As we swam around the other side and land came back into view, my sister began screaming for help. By this point my survival instincts set in, and I locked in to the shore. I had the searing realization that I could die in this water. There was an urgency to make it to land or die trying, which I had never-before experienced. In swimming back toward shore my sister told me to use her to stay afloat as needed. I would desperately swim a few strokes, and then grab onto her for a rest.

I was over six feet tall and much heavier than my sister, yet she selflessly allowed me to weigh her down as I fought to stay at the surface.

Thankfully, a man who appeared smaller than me swam out towards us. I knew my sister was exhausted from holding me up, so I threw my weight onto the man. He was trying to calm me down as we continued moving toward shore, but I kept thrashing away, wasting energy and fatiguing him as well.

Finally, a couple on a green kayak approached us and my focus shifted from the shore which was still about 40 meters away to the green God-send ten meters away. I remember seeing the man hop into the water while the woman stayed on; both helped me to lie across the kayak. Sensing my sister next to me, I closed my eyes, thanking God and waiting for the feel of sand. When I opened my eyes, we were coming to shore; it was still a beautiful day, but something in me had changed.

I never was able to give proper thanks to those three angels who came to our aid, so my hope is that the remainder of my life is me paying it forward by helping others.

To this day, my sister hates talking about that episode. She truly saved my life, and I know she doesn't like thinking about almost losing her brother. I think there is a part of me that will always be in the waters around that trampoline. Thinking about that situation gives me sincere gratitude and a sense of urgency because I know that save for the selflessness and quick-thinking of my sister and three strangers, I would not be alive today.

We slowly returned to our room and as I took a shower and listened to T.I's Paper Trail album, I reflected on my face-to-face experience with my mortality. My parents eventually arrived at the room, and we explained to them what had happened. I remember feeling hesitant to tell them about the day's events and there being a thick graveness as we sat there.

Unbeknownst to me, my parents had already scheduled us for a boating expedition complete with snorkeling in the salty seawater for the following day. I remember feeling terrified to get back into the water; the salty water had recently left my mouth but not my mind.

It took every ounce of mental and emotional power to force myself into the water and not stay on the boat the following day. I remember thinking, *If I do not get back into the water now, I won't be back in for a long time.* So, with my life jacket on, and my snorkeling gear in hand, I dropped into the water. My body froze as I tasted the saltwater, and it took me the next thirty minutes to feel somewhat comfortable in the water. The rest of the trip was amazing, but in the back of my mind I knew that trip could have ended in tragedy.

In the ensuing years, I spent plenty of time in pools and lakes with friends, but little time in saltwater. Fast-forward to

2015 when some friends and I decided to get our scuba certification while we were living on the beautiful island of Okinawa. Obtaining a scuba certification involves classroom instruction, exhibiting both swimming and water-treading capabilities, and multiple dives in the open water with a certified instructor.

The first time we entered the open water for our first full-gear scuba dive, I tasted the saltwater and reflected on my experience in Mexico in 2008, my life since then, and my current excitement to be in the water. As we descended that first time, a whole new world appeared. Everyone sees the surface of the water, but once you get below the surface with the right equipment, you see the beauty and grandeur of the ocean. There is abundant life below the surface. I was not equipped nor interested in seeing the subsurface that summer day near the water trampoline in 2008. I emerged from the water that day in 2015 thankful for life and the opportunity to experience the serenity and beauty of the water.

Resilience is great to have, takes time to build, and sucks to need. If you need resilience, it usually means you are experiencing adversity: rejection, a poor grade, the ending of a relationship, unemployment, the death of a loved one, a near-death experience.

I purposely begin this book with the *Resilience* Section because it is prudent to have a proper view of yourself, an accurate inventory of your unique abilities and qualities, a proper understanding of stewardship as it applies to your life, and a keen awareness that life comes with challenges.

ADVERSITY

Adversity: a state or instance of serious or continued difficulty or misfortune.[7]

Adversity is the tension to resilience. Without adversity, resilience would not be so vital. In fact, resilience can be defined as being the capacity to recover from difficulties. Living life without adversity is a fairytale. (And even fairytales usually have the protagonist encounter difficulties.) Adversity is a normal part of life. I don't want to minimize the gravity of your current situation; rather, I want to expose you to this idea and hopefully encourage and equip you to move in and through your situation.

If you are not currently facing an adverse situation, sooner or later, you will encounter adversity in some form. The question becomes, can we prepare for adversity? Can we increase our capacity to recover quickly from difficulties? I believe we can. More than my belief, research conducted at the Penn Resilience Program shows that many aspects of resilience are teachable. The remainder of this section, and this book, will hopefully provide some tools and lessons to grow your resilience.

Recovering quickly from adversity does not mean we won't experience pain, denial, sadness, anger, inadequacy, depression, and frustration at times. These feelings are also important to be aware of, acknowledge, and process appropriately.

Adversity is not created equal. And our responses may differ depending on the severity of the adversity. And truthfully, not all adversity is bad. Adversity can be a catalyst for change.

It demands action. Either forward progress and improvement, or downward decline, degradation, and despair.

The concepts and tools below are even more important when you are facing adversity. I purposely begin the *Resilience* Section with Adversity because it is imperative that you are aware that you will encounter difficult times at some point in your life. If you are unprepared for those adverse times, or do not believe they will ever arrive, it will make the difficult situation worse. This first section is too important to skip.

"Do you realize how many events,
choices, that had to occur since the birth
of the universe leading to the making
of you just exactly the way you are?"
Ms. Which, A Wrinkle in Time

PURPOSE

This was not in the original draft of Enduring Urgency. It took me being patient with and trusting my own process to realize that living with Enduring Urgency requires you to search for, understand, and operate in your purpose. Urgency means *importance requiring swift action*. Importance. What is important to you? In order to know what is important to you, you must first know who you are, what you love, what you fear, what excites you, what gives you pleasure.

What is the importance that I believe requires my swift action? You. Encouraging, educating, and equipping you to live with Enduring Urgency is important to me. Loving and uniting people are important to me. Exposing people to the idea that compassion, unity, and collaboration are more powerful and enduring than apathy, division, and hate is important to me.

This understanding of my purpose did not come overnight or all at once. It took time, effort, and intentionality. Understanding I have purpose is the cornerstone of me living with Enduring Urgency. So, I start with this truth: You are here on purpose. Be intentional with your day, with your relationships, with your energy. It is not an accident that you came across this book at this time. You may have received it from a friend, you may have discovered it online, or you may have come across it in an old bookstore. This book is part of your purpose.

It is not an accident that you are here at this point in human history. The quote by Ms. Which captures this truth.

"Do you realize how many events, choices that had to occur since the birth of the universe leading to the making of you just exactly the way you are?"[8]

When I first heard this question posed while watching *A Wrinkle in Time*, I pulled out my phone in the middle of the theater because it was too important to forget. (Yes, I went to see *A Wrinkle in Time* at the movie theater by myself.) If this question seems irrelevant because you have never questioned your purpose, then I am glad. For me, it was a process to figure out what I am meant to do in life. It did not happen overnight, and to be honest, I cannot say I have it all figured out. What I am sure of is how critical it is to discover your purpose, your why, your reason for getting up each morning. For some, it is their family. For others it is their vocation. For others, it is a deep desire within them to maximize every opportunity, ability, and idea they have.

STEWARDSHIP

Scientific Definition of Resilience: The capability of a strained body to recover its size and shape after deformation caused especially by compressive stress.

When talking about resilience, it is prudent to discuss stewardship, which encapsulates responsibility, accountability, and even blame.

Imagine holding a spring between your thumb and pointer finger and then compressing the spring until your fingers are almost touching. You then release the spring and it returns to its original shape and size. One scientific definition of resilience is "the capability of a strained body to recover its size and shape after deformation caused especially by compressive stress". The strained body (read: the spring) did not deform itself; rather, its deformation was caused by an exterior force.

Warning: Resilience is not merely about who or what caused the strained body to be deformed. To focus solely on what led to the deformation is to discredit the ability of the strained body to recover from the compressive stress, which misses the power of resilience. Likewise, to deny what caused the strained body to be deformed is dismissive, and implies a misunderstanding of the complete definition of resilience. Put another way: To focus solely on what led you to your current situation, is to discredit your ability to move forward, which minimizes the power of your resilience and the power you have to improve your future. Likewise, to deny the factors and actions that have impacted you is to downplay reality, and implies a misunderstanding of the complete definition of resilience.

"Life is 10% what happens to you and 90% how you react to it."

- Charles R. Swindoll[9]

The percentages may not be exact, but I agree with the premise. Stewardship is how we respond and interact with our situations in life, which determines the extent to which we live. Understanding I am responsible for my life and my future empowers me to take the focused action necessary to improve myself. Understanding there are exterior factors at work (laws, institutions, biases, etc.) increases my awareness and encourages me to be patient as I take consistent focused action within my sphere of influence.

We have each been given unique abilities, ideas, and opportunities. It is up to you to determine what those will become. We have the responsibility to be good stewards of the abilities, ideas, and opportunities we have been given.

Stewardship is the activity or job of protecting, improving, and being responsible for something. Being responsible can be empowering. You may not be solely responsible for where you are today, but you are responsible for YOUR response and YOUR future from this point forward.

This is not to discount what you are currently experiencing in your life. As you steward this life you have been given; as you work to learn yourself, grow your abilities to skills, and develop your knowledge into know-how, you will be better able to handle the adversity in your life and operate effectively within your sphere of influence. Tim Grover, author of *Relentless* and an experienced trainer of elite athletes such as Michael Jordan and Kobe Bryant, puts it another way. "It's not selfish to focus on improving yourself. The more you improve, the better you can take care of all those important people counting on you today."[10]

You are here on purpose.
It is not an accident.
So, live on purpose.
Be deliberate and diligent with
your time, energy, and relationships.
And, live in purpose.
Steward well your opportunities,
talents, ideas, and time.

The Garden

We've each been given a garden, with fertile soil and seeds planted in the soil. I believe those seeds are gifts from God. It takes time to figure out what those seeds will become. In order to see the harvest of the seeds, we must diligently and consistently water them, ensure they are getting the required sunlight, and be wary of weeds.

The catch is we don't initially know which seeds are plants and which are weeds. It takes time and focused effort to fully understand your garden. Too often, we get caught up focusing on our neighbors' gardens rather than taking care of our own. We can ask questions, learn gardening strategies from our neighbors, even borrow gardening tools, but we can't expect to do the exact same thing in our garden because what is in our garden is not the same as what is in their garden. This is stewardship.

Just as you cannot completely control how much sunlight, rain, or wind comes to your garden, there will be factors in your life that you cannot control. Focus on your sphere of influence. Tend to your garden. Steward it well and it will grow.

I dare you to use this book to improve yourself. It will take honest reflection, a willingness to make changes, and action. The next few topics are meant to lead you in that direction. Let's continue!

What's in Your Garden? What abilities, ideas, and opportunities have you been given?

IDENTITY, IDENTIFICATION, AND INVENTORY

As part of stewardship and tending your garden, it is important to know what is in your garden, to know where you are starting. Before you can focus on what is important to you, it is important to know who you are. This is what I mean by identity. So, who are you?

This question was a challenge to me because for the past five years exclusively, and much of the last ten years, I tied a large portion of my identity to my military service. As I transitioned out of the United States Air Force into business school, I had to redefine who I was outside of the uniform. It is a challenge that military members face when retiring or separating from the military. It is also a challenge many of my classmates have faced as they've transitioned from their careers into business school. I initially thought it was a problem unique to me; however, as business school started and I talked to more of my classmates, I realized this question is bigger than me. This question *"Who am I?"* is a human question. I don't think it is a question you ask yourself once and then never have to answer again. I believe it is an important question to ask yourself regularly and whenever you are transitioning.

I identified who I thought I was, took inventory of my strengths and weaknesses, and identified what I wanted to focus on developing and improving to get to the person I want to be. This is the Enduring Urgency mindset: always learning and working to improve, knowing it will take time and you will face challenges.

I took inventory of my strengths and weaknesses. But it was deeper than that. I took inventory of my habits and researched where my family comes from.

Identity is powerful. I liken life to being dropped in the middle of a forest. There is currently a show called *Naked and Afraid*. In it, two contestants are taken to a relatively obscure area of the earth, typically a jungle or desert, with a map, one tool each, and instructions of where they need to get to in the next 21 days in order to be picked up. Besides that, yes, they are naked.

Now, imagine being taken and dropped in the middle of forest you have never been in. You do not have a map; you do not have someone telling you where you are nor where you need to go. As your survival instincts kick in, maybe you look for drinkable water, food, and shelter. Beyond that, you may wander (seemingly aimlessly) until you come across another person, civilization, or a predator. Your chances of survival are adequate at best.

Now, imagine being given a map or GPS that indicates where you are on the map and where certain landmarks are. The power of identity is the difference between moving through that forest with a map versus without.

The contestants on *Naked and Afraid* are given a map with hazardous areas together with their extraction point identified. They still have to work together and survive (i.e. find water, secure food, make shelter), but their chances of survival are greatly increased because they know where they are and where they need to go. I'm bringing it back to the topic: your chances of survival/impact/effectiveness are much greater if you know who you are (Identity), know what you have (Inventory), and know where you want to go and what you need to get there (Identification). This principle is true whether you are in a forest, in life, or in business.

As you do the work of identity, identification, and inventory, you become more resilient, better understand your process, and are better enabled to take consistent focused action in the things that are important to you.

So, who are you?

AUTHENTICITY

There is abundance in authenticity. Abundance of peace, abundance of clarity, abundance of self-love. You must know yourself, your strengths, and your weaknesses; and knowing yourself takes time and effort. A few years ago, I went through the process of finding myself. And truthfully, I am still going through my self-discovery and self-growth process. To me, it is a process that lasts a lifetime. Becoming aware of your abilities, your opportunities to improve, your true desires, and your fears takes time and effort. If you don't know who you are, you can't truly love yourself, you can't live an authentic life, and you will not know what you need in a partner.

I am not an expert on relationships, but I wonder if many relationships struggle because one or both individuals do not know themselves and thus do not know and are not able to articulate what they want and need from their partner.

For me, it was easier to write everything out. In putting my thoughts on paper, I was able to decipher my true thoughts and emotions about myself. And then I started the process of building myself up and turning my abilities into skills and my knowledge into know-how.

Authenticity is a key component of resilience. Knowing yourself and being true to yourself enables you to process mistakes as lessons and operate in a more liberated capacity.

Today, we tend to want to emulate those we see on social media. The do-it-all moms, the shredded athletes, the beautiful models, the wisdom-filled moguls.

Social media has many benefits and I use it daily. Yet, I believe social media can be a disservice to authenticity. I have caught myself getting lost in social media; seeing someone doing what I want to do and becoming discouraged; or simply wasting time avoiding working on projects (like this book). Don't worry! We'll discuss distractions in Section 3.

At the same time, social media has enabled many people to express their authenticity in their own way, which is encouraging to witness. The opportunities for building an authentic platform have progressed since the turn of the century: from Myspace and YouTube to Facebook and Vine to Instagram and Snapchat.

There is abundance in authenticity. YOU have unique abilities, and the world needs you to use them. Today. Dr. Dharius Daniels, pastor of Change Church, says, "Humans have something other species in the created order do not have. We have the gift of an amazing mind. It is an invaluable gift from God. We possess a thinking capacity that is absolutely unparalleled."[11] And no two minds are the same.

You must be willing to imagine who you can be, imagine all you can do. And then do the work required to develop your abilities into skills and your knowledge into know-how. If you are willing to do that, abundance awaits. In today's world the word abundance is typically equated with money. I am referring to more than monetary abundance.

I mean abundance of peace, abundance of self-love, abundance of clarity, abundance of healthy relationships, abundance of resources. The process is not easy, but it is worth it.

My challenge to you is this: Be authentic. Be the best you, you can be. Be a good steward of your life. Do the work required to develop your abilities into skills and your knowledge into know-how. And then work to improve them. That's the process. I heard another gentleman put it this way: "There is a traffic jam in the lanes of conformity. But there is acceleration in authenticity." If you get in your own lane, you accelerate as you operate with an enduring sense of urgency because there is no one in front of you.

Authenticity and stewardship are inextricably linked. You have a responsibility to understand your abilities and knowledge. As a good steward, put in the work required to turn those abilities into skills and the knowledge into know-how. I've used this phrase multiple times now because living with authenticity and stewardship is a process which takes patience; we will discuss *Patience* and *The Process* further in Section Two.

INTEGRITY

Integrity is not perfection; it is excellent authenticity. It is important to reframe your mind about what is a mistake, what is failure, and what is not. Even with resilience, patience, and consistent focused action, you will make mistakes. Knowing this hopefully saves you hours, if not days of anguish, frustration, and anxiety. Doing things with integrity does not mean you will not make mistakes; it in fact almost guarantees that you will make mistakes. You are a human, and humans are imperfect creatures. As you operate in your own authentic way, you will inevitably make mistakes. And that is okay.

I was an Air Advisor during my last assignment in the United States Air Force. In that position, I would lead multi-disciplinary teams to countries across Africa to build relationships with and the capabilities of our partner nation air forces. Our teams would work with our counterparts in the US Embassies in these countries to ensure we were delivering the desired training to our partners. At the end of one of our engagements, our team visited the in-country embassy to meet with our stakeholders and share with them the training and advising we had conducted and our recommendations.

This was seen as an important part of the mission and we worked to ensure we presented ourselves as the experienced professionals we were. As we began the meeting, I introduced our team and as I thought ahead to the important information I wanted to convey, I blanked on the name of one of my team members and friends. I recovered, apologized, and the remainder of the meeting was productive but I was both embarrassed and guilty that I had erred in such an important moment. My assistant laughed about it afterwards but also recommended that I simply let everyone introduce themselves in the future.

Integrity is not perfection; it is excellent authenticity. This idea is about doing things well, acknowledging if and when you err, and working to make sure that that specific error does NOT happen again. Mistakes happens; it's part of doing, learning, and growing. And since I hope to continue doing, learning, and growing, I must understand that errors are part of the process.

Repeat this to yourself daily
and mean it:

I CAN ONLY <u>DO</u> WHAT I CAN <u>DO</u>
AND
ONLY I CAN <u>DO</u> WHAT I CAN <u>DO</u>,
SO
I WILL <u>DO</u> WHAT I CAN <u>DO</u>
IN EXCELLENCE.

1ST PART SPEAKS TO KNOWING YOURSELF AND KNOWING
YOUR SPHERE OF INFLUENCE AND OPERATING WITHIN IT.
2ND PART SPEAKS TO PURPOSE AND THE FACT THAT YOU
HAVE BEEN UNIQUELY EQUIPPED TO DO WHAT YOU WERE
PLACED ON THIS EARTH TO DO.
3RD PART IS A DECISION TO USE YOUR UNIQUE TALENTS AND
ABILITIES TO OPERATE WITHIN YOUR SPHERE OF INFLUENCE
WITH A MIND AND HEART IN EXCELLENCE.

COMPARISON

As you strive to live excellently in your own authenticity, I urge you to avoid comparison. One of the most iconic pictures to me is from the 2016 Olympics and captures a race where Michael Phelps is dialed in to the final stroke of his race, while one of his opponents has his head turned and is looking at Phelps to gauge his status in the race. I believe that comparison is one of the most demotivating, distracting, and deleterious pastimes you can have. Instead, focus on your own abilities and set goals that allow you to grow in skills and know-how.

I want to ensure you do not misinterpret what I am saying: you can learn from other people. If you do watch others, take up a learning and celebrating posture. Again, there is abundance in authenticity. You can celebrate someone else, learn from them, and apply those lessons learned to your own life. Sometimes, watching others exposes us to new ideas. In that sense, you are winning because you are learning. Be mindful to avoid the creeping feeling of comparison that may give way to jealousy.

MISTAKES AND FAILURE

"I have failed many times. And that is why I succeed."
– Michael Jordan[12]

I make mistakes. I fail. I wrote this section after I just failed miserably at executing a promotion ceremony for a fellow engineer. He asked me to be the emcee at his promotion ceremony, which is both a big honor and big responsibility. I misread the script and mistimed the narration multiple times. Much of my failure in this instance was due to a lack of communication, which we will discuss later in this section, and lack of preparation, which we will discuss more in depth in Section 2. I did not ask enough questions to understand the full scope of the task. I was frustrated because I knew he and his family deserved a better ceremony, and I was frustrated because I was unaware of the extent of the requirements.

I want you to do three things when you experience failure or make a mistake. First, embrace the pain and disappointment. If that means getting upset or crying for a few minutes, do that. Second, understand why you didn't reach your goal. This is the toughest part because it forces you to be honest with yourself and acknowledge areas you need to improve in. Third, remember those feelings of pain, disappointment, and embarrassment so that when you are working on your next goal you have an extra bit of fire to push through.

Now this sounds great on paper but is admittedly harder to put into practice. I wish I could tell you that by living with Enduring Urgency you will avoid mistakes and disappointment. I can't and I won't. I will tell that living with Enduring Urgency will lead to personal growth and progress in those things that are important to you. Mistakes, challenges, and setbacks will occur. Knowing this is critical. How do you move forward?

COURAGE

This is where courage comes in. Finding yourself, stewarding your abilities and opportunities, and living authentically takes work. People may doubt you. People may discourage you. People may ridicule you. But, as you live in your authentic self, you become more confident because you know who you are.

Friends and even family may not understand where you are coming from in moving through life the way you are. Gift them this book.

Christmas 2017 was the first Christmas in four years I was able to spend at home with my family due to my military service. One morning I was home with my little sister, Shemilore, and talking to my mom as she prepared to head in to work. My mom is currently a judge in California. Prior to being appointed, she was a family law attorney with her own practice. The subject of our conversation that morning was building a vision from the ground up, and specifically the book SOAR by Bishop T.D. Jakes. She shared with me in detail the process by which she came to the United States from England, became an attorney, and eventually opened her own family law practice.

That previous sentence captures twenty years of hard work, learning, failure, faith, resilience, patience, and consistent focused action. I asked her how she continued to push forward at some of the most crucial moments in her journey. She responded with her faith in God and her belief in her vision. She said, "Don't let your fear keep you from your future. Feel the fear and act anyway." This may be the singular concept you need to move forward.

She understood it would take time, energy, and focus to reach her goals; she understood there would be difficult times, especially being an ocean away from her family; she learned that courage does not mean never being afraid, but acting despite your fear. And her life is a testimony to courage in the face of adversity and living life with Enduring Urgency.

I don't know what you are experiencing in your life as you read these words. You are a human. There is a reason you are reading this book. And if it is solely for you to read these words, let me say them clearly: Feel the fear of being your authentic self, feel the fear of being inadequate, feel the fear of setting goals to improve yourself, feel the fear of acting in pursuit of your purpose, feel the fear of making mistakes. Feel the fear, and act anyway. Do not let your fear keep you from your future.

Reminder:
"DON'T LET YOUR FEAR
KEEP YOU FROM YOUR FUTURE.
FEEL THE FEAR
AND ACT ANYWAY."
- My mom, Bunmi Brown-Dawson

Depression

I could not write a book about resilience without addressing depression and how prevalent it is. I'm not an expert on this subject, but I have had my struggles with depression and I have friends who have allowed me inside their own struggles with depression. I hope that even by talking about it here, we can break this stigma surrounding depression and hopefully prevent someone from taking their own life.

In the summer of 2010, I was home in California visiting family, hanging out with friends, and celebrating the new high school graduates. It was during one of those graduation parties that we received news that a former classmate had committed suicide. In the subsequent minutes and days many of us were stunned and had few words except astonishment and utter disbelief. Marcus' story hit me hard in the days that followed because of how big he seemed throughout high school. See, Marcus was an exceptional athlete and confident in his abilities. He was a year older than me and I admired his abilities on both the football field and the track.

At the time of his death, he had been out of high school for all of two years. Looking back, we thought we were so old. He had been going through a tough time with his girlfriend among other problems. Amid the intensity of his problems, he chose to end his life. He left behind his parents, siblings, and two beautiful nieces. Sadly, Marcus's story has occurred in cities and towns all over the country.

His death forced me to acknowledge that everyone struggles at times – no matter their stature or accomplishments.

Two of my favorite artists, Lecrae and Tori Kelly, collaborated and made a song in 2017 called "I'll Find You". As I listened for the first time, I thought about Marcus and others who were going through a tough time. It reminded me of my own past struggles with depression, which I talk more in depth about in *Date Yourself*, part of the *Patience* Section.

One of my friends from high school lives with chronic depression. I asked him if I could share some of our conversations for this project and he graciously agreed. Part of his life's work is to help other people dealing with depression, open the conversation about depression, and reduce the stigma around people who deal with depression. I have learned that there are levels to depression; and I wanted to discuss this topic within the realm of resilience because I know even though my friend suffers from chronic depression, he has increased his ability to recover quickly from the regular difficulties brought on by chronic depression. He is resilient because he is *living* with depression.

Hurting Heroes

I was having a conversation with several of my military coworkers and the topic of therapy came up. I listened as a couple of them shared their story of their struggles and how they decided to seek out help in the form of therapy to improve their situations. At the time I wasn't aware of many people who had had therapy, and I expressed surprise at their willingness to discuss it.

One of them told me he was sharing in the hope that people might be encouraged to act and receive the help they needed and deserved. Instead of reaching out, we sometimes try to solve and deal with issues on our own. We might hesitate to ask for help for any number of reasons: pride, shame, what we've been taught and exposed to, and through devaluing our situation. We should eliminate any perceived stigma around depression and therapy. Instead, we should encourage our loved ones who need therapy to seek it and we ourselves should seek it as needed.

Having served alongside some of the most selfless and bravest people, it is apparent that resilience runs deep within these heroes and their families. The atrocities some have had to see, the actions some have had to take, and the nightmares some have had to endure should be intentionally discussed and wholly addressed.

We need more focused resources and treatment; more love and understanding. We must discuss seeking assistance in a more positive light and support those who ask for it.

Sometimes, we devalue our difficulties by calling them "first-world problems". This can paralyze us from seeking assistance because we feel that our problems are illegitimate. I must be mindful even now to avoid thinking that to myself, or saying that in response to a friend or colleague sharing a personal issue with me. I think we can remind ourselves of our blessings without reducing or devaluing the stress and emotions we are feeling at a given time.

FACTS, FAITH, AND GOD

It took a special day for me to write this section. I was avoiding including anything about God in this book so as not to put people off. The fact is my faith in God *is* the major key to my approach to life. In the past few months, I have had people wonder why I am as positive and energetic as I am. To the extent they hypothesized it was due to performance enhancing drugs. I laughed it off but neglected to share with them the real reason, in part because I never want to push my beliefs on anyone. That said, this project would be incomplete if I did not acknowledge my personal relationship with God and how it has kept me through some of the toughest moments in my life.

I love writing because it forces me to address my true thoughts, feelings, and perspectives on certain topics. I consider myself a pragmatic optimist; and I have become more comfortable acknowledging that I operate with facts rooted in faith. Faith is confidence in what we hope for and assurance about what we do not see.

I have faith that the airplane I am on will get me to my destination. I did not design the plane, nor did I conduct its maintenance, nor am I the one flying it. Yet still, I have faith that the people who designed, maintained, and fly the plane are qualified and produced a plane that will get me to my destination.

Similarly, I did not create this universe, nor did I design the world as it currently is; Yet still, I have faith that the creator of the universe created me on purpose and for a purpose. If I had designed, maintained, and flew the plane I would not necessarily need faith because to a certain degree I was in control and I had the facts of the plane's air worthiness. Similarly, if I had designed the universe and created all that is, I would not need faith in what is to come because I would already know as the designer. I operate with facts rooted in faith. Faith rooted in facts is not faith at all.

One of my favorite authors is Jim Collins, and a few years ago I read his book *Good to Great*. In his book, he discusses an interview he did with Admiral James Stockdale, a Vietnam veteran and prisoner of war for eight years. In it, Admiral Stockdale discusses the need to confront the brutal facts of your situation and maintain faith that you can and will overcome them.

Admiral Stockdale states, "You must never confuse faith that you will prevail in the end—which you can never afford to lose—with the discipline to confront the most brutal facts of your current reality, whatever they might be."[13]

I believe he operated with pragmatic optimism and with Enduring Urgency. Faith in the long-term outcome, willingness to acknowledge the facts of his immediate surroundings, a sense of urgency to do whatever it took to get home.

Prior to entering active duty, I was blessed with the opportunity to work for former US Congressman Sam Johnson. He, like Mr. Stockdale, spent many years as a prisoner of war during the Vietnam War. In his book, *Captive Warriors*, Johnson discusses how his faith in God, his love for his family, and his belief in his country enabled him to survive austere conditions as a prisoner of war.

Side note: Johnson's life impacted me for many reasons. He continued to serve in the military after he returned from the war in Vietnam. Once he retired, Johnson spent some time in business ventures then decided to serve his community and country as a congressman because he saw public office as a way he could help improve his country. He could have retired from the US Air Force and lived out the remainder of his life with his family as an American hero. Instead, he chose to continue serving faithfully in another capacity.

"What More Do You Want?"

I must be careful to not allow my faith to paralyze me from taking swift action in my life.

I am reminded of the story of the man trapped on his roof during a flood. A neighbor came by on a rowboat and offered to take him to safety. The man responded, "Don't worry about me. I have faith God will save me." So, the neighbor continued on. The water continued to rise. A family in a motorboat stopped by and offered a seat on their boat as they were heading to safety. The man responded, "Give that seat to someone else. I have faith God will save me." The family reluctantly continued on. The water rose to the man's feet as he was standing on the roof. A helicopter came by and extended a ladder along with a rescue officer to save him. The man repeatedly turned down the rescue officer's help saying, "I have faith God will save me." Realizing the futility of his efforts, the rescue officer and the helicopter left the man. Soon after, the man drowned. When he reached heaven, he had the opportunity to talk to God. "I had faith you would save me. Why did you not come and save me?" God responded, "I sent you a man in a rowboat, a family in a motorboat, and a rescue officer on a helicopter. What more did you want?"

There are times when my faith has kept me from the practical help in front of me. I work to strike a balance:

maintaining my faith in God, acknowledging the resources he has placed around me, and doing my part to best steward those resources (read: to make the most of those opportunities). Bishop T.D. Jakes says it this way: God doesn't make chairs, he makes trees. It is our responsibility to take those trees and make them into tables, chairs, cabinets, houses.

On the specific subject of mental health, there are therapists and counselors who are trained and willing to listen and help work through your problems. For some reason, talking about mental health and therapists has been a taboo subject in parts of our culture. That needs to change.

My faith is deeply personal to me. I think your relationship with God or belief in a higher power is just that, yours. That said, leaving this part out of the Enduring Urgency formula and this book would have been a mistake and a disservice.

COMMUNICATION

When I was living in Okinawa, I ran a marathon on what was later determined to be a torn meniscus. My buddy, David, and I committed ourselves with a high-five over Thanksgiving dinner that we would run a marathon in February. The next three months were a true test of resilience, patience, and consistent focused action. We knew we had relatively little time to prepare for our marathon with Christmas, New Year's, traveling, and all the holiday food coming up fast. But we made a commitment to each other and we held each other accountable; we were accountabilibuddies. One thing that cannot be overstated is the difference a teammate makes in working towards a goal, in living with Enduring Urgency.

We worked our way up from three-mile runs to a twenty-mile run in the weeks leading up to the actual marathon day. I missed a few of the preparation runs mainly because my knee would swell up. Some days I pushed through and other days I chose to rest it. The marathon was exhausting and painful, yet exhilarating.

It wasn't until later that year as I was preparing to get surgery to repair my meniscus that I told David about missing some runs due to my knee. His response was funny and enlightening. "I thought you were just being a baby about not wanting to run. I didn't know you were running on a torn meniscus. Wow!"

His perception of me immediately shifted when I shared that information. He went from thinking I had been simply slacking on the preparation to being amazed I ran and did as well as I did on a bum knee. I share this story to remind you of the importance of communication. Communicating your situation, struggles and all, with someone you trust is critical. I chose not to share it with him because I did not want him to think I was wimping out and using my knee as an excuse. I didn't realize he would have been more understanding and supportive if I had shared my pain with him. Fast-forward to post-surgery, he and his wife, Marie, brought me food and checked up on me repeatedly.

While writing this book, I read the book *Option B* by Sheryl Sandberg and Adam Grant. The subtitle of the book captures its theme: *Facing Adversity, Building Resilience, and Finding Joy.* In it, Sheryl discusses the sudden passing of her husband and life after his death. She also discusses the community that she built in which people dealing with adversity can find others who are dealing with similar situations.

After reading this book, I wrote a letter to my dad telling him how the book gave me insight into his situation following the death of my biological mom, Genevieve, when I was three years old. In the past few years we have had deeper discussions about his life growing up in Sierra Leone, coming to America, and life after my mom Genevieve passed away from breast cancer, and before he married my mom Bunmi. The more we talk, the more I appreciate my dad, his decisions, his sacrifices, and his resilience. His stories allow me context into decisions he has made, goals he has had, and his approach to life.

My dad's life is a testimony to resilience, selflessness, and love in the face of adversity, and living life with Enduring Urgency. Turns out we, his children, were the important things requiring his swift and consistent action. My dad is my hero.

BE GENEROUS

Identifying generosity as a component of resilience may seem out of place but stay with me. And think not just in terms of money, but in terms of time, energy, and love. When you choose to serve others or provide a service to others in your unique way, you are operating from a mindset of abundance.

I believe in the law of attraction and it has showed itself many times over the past few years. Because I enjoy reading so much, I began giving out specific books to friends that had a major impact on my life. One was *The Circle Maker* by Mark Batterson, another was *Linchpin* by Seth Godin, and another was *EntreLeadership* by Dave Ramsey. The more books I gave away, the more people recommended books to me, people sent books to me, or I came across a book at just the right time.

I met with a coworker early in 2018 who had served in the military for 21 years and was preparing to retire. I asked him on the fly if we could sit down for a mentoring session sometime in the next few weeks before he left. Literally 30 minutes later he found me, and we went to his office to talk. Be generous.

I had prepared a few questions. I really wanted to glean from him how to better serve, but I understood that he still had obligations to tend to prior to his retirement. Still, we talked for about 30 minutes and he answered all my questions and then some. He gave of himself freely and openly and as a result I was more aware of how to meet the needs of my team.

Two of the takeaways from our mentoring session: One, be generous. Very few people have jobs where we cannot take five minutes to help someone. You never know who you can help, and you never know the impact that person may have because of your help. Two, do not be afraid to ask for help. My position as an Air Advisor had me in a constant state of question-asking. Consequently, it had me in a constant state of learning and growth. It amazes me how willing people are to help and share their wisdom if we are simply willing to ask.

There is an interesting consequence of gleaning from people who are willing to mentor me. I have a desire to push myself and help as many people as possible. Bishop T.D. Jakes captures it when he says, "Glean up, share across, teach down." Which is why I am writing this. Near the end of our conversation, I asked my coworker what words he lives by. His response: Be generous.

Life is truly about the people we meet, the impact that people have on us, and how we can have a positive impact on others. How can you be generous with what you have where you are now? It could be an encouraging word or note to someone, a check-in phone call, a helping hand, a meal. Feel free to use this page to write down a few ideas.

How can you be generous?

CHOICE

Life is determined by the choices we make. As discussed earlier in this section, there are other factors that can impact our life, but we have the ability and responsibility to choose our approach to life.

Resilience is one of the three tenants of Enduring Urgency because life is not always easy. We each have our issues, setbacks, and concerns; this mindset will not magically fix your problems overnight. You may even have to deal with some negative consequences of your own actions or the actions of others. It will take time, energy, and intentionality. But, from this day forward you can work to build your resilience. Here are of some of the ways:

- ❖ Be a good steward of your abilities and knowledge and put in the required work to turn your abilities into skills and knowledge into know-how.
- ❖ Live authentically, understand your strengths and weaknesses, and continue to learn.
- ❖ Choose a problem in your world to solve and work to solve it.
- ❖ Avoid comparison, and instead learn from and celebrate people around you.
- ❖ View mistakes and failures as life lessons rather than proof of your incompetence and unworthiness.
- ❖ Be generous with your time, energy, and life experience.
- ❖ Express gratitude for what you currently have, even if it is as simple as air to breathe.

Yes, these are all choices. You can choose to do these things daily. Being resilient is a choice. We are usually more resilient than we think. We as human beings are born with resilience and based on certain exterior factors, some people are forced to utilize and thus build and employ that resilience sooner than others. Implementing the actions discussed in this section can help you build your resilience.

NOTES

YOUR GIFTS ARE GIVEN.
HOW YOU STEWARD YOUR
GIFTS IS YOUR CHOICE
AND WILL DETERMINE
THE QUALITY AND
COURSE OF YOUR LIFE.

SECTION II: PATIENCE

Patience: the ability to accept or tolerate delays, problems, or suffering without becoming annoyed or anxious.[14]

After graduating from Texas Tech University with a degree in civil engineering and commissioning into the US Air Force on December 14, 2013, I entered my "survive-and-don't-get-in-trouble" phase. This is what we called the period of time between commissioning and leaving for our first active duty station. During this period, we are not paid nor do we have any daily requirements related to the Air Force. I did not know how long I would have to wait until I started active duty. It ended up being over nine months. In hindsight they were some of the most fulfilling and enlightening months of my life, but I was initially concerned as to how that time would unfold.

Prior to my graduation, I was accepted into and had committed to participating in the Congressional Internship Program that Texas Tech has with US Congressmen representing districts across Texas. I told the organizers of the program that I may get called onto active duty with short notice, and they graciously worked with me.

Over the first five months of 2014, I met many intelligent and passionate people, learned a lot about our government and public service, and worked for a man who taught me that service to your country extends beyond serving in the military. After my five months in DC, I went back to Texas to pack up my belongings in preparation for my first assignment and then headed to California to spend a few months with my family. While I was at home, I worked as a Quality Assurance Analyst for Blue Shield of California. It was here I learned another method of project management that I would only fully understand and appreciate during my time in the military. I also met some amazingly talented individuals and learned about an industry I had previously known little about.

Finally, I was sitting in my car in the parking lot of Blue Shield during lunch one day, when I came up with the idea of DICEi: Delivering Ideas that Change Everything, Inc. I'll discuss it more towards the end of this book, in *Cross-Community Collaboration*. A few weeks later I was having dinner with my high school buddy, Derik, and I shared the idea with him. They say the first follower turns a crazy person into a leader.

I share this period of my life with you for two reasons. One, there was a lot of patience involved in surviving and not getting into trouble, and I tried to make the most of the time I had. In doing so, I met new people, learned new skills, and was exposed to new ideas. Two, each of us progresses in our own timing. Over the course of this section, we will discuss active patience as part of living life with Enduring Urgency.

There is power in learning patience. Just like resilience, patience is a skill that can be developed. A misnomer about patience is to correlate it with inaction. Patience is consistently investing in your growth, your knowledge, your awareness, your community. I heard Michael Todd, leader of Transformation Church in Tulsa, Oklahoma, say, "Patience is answering the question: How are you waiting?" He then took a towel, placed it over his arm to look like a waiter, and repeated, "How are you *waiting*?"

He was encouraging the listeners to reflect on how they were serving. So, I will ask you: How are you serving? How are you serving others? Are you serving others by building yourself, developing your skills, increasing your value so you can be of value to others when they need you?

Developing patience is not easy, which is one reason it is so important to begin this book with resilience. Your own process will not happen overnight, and it will have its ups and some downs. It is how you use the seemingly insignificant time to grow in knowledge of self, find clarity of purpose, and develop your skills which will ultimately shape where you go and how you are in life.

You don't plant the seed and
eat the fruit on the same day.
But that does not mean
you should not plant the seed.

THE PROCESS

During the early phases of writing this section, I came across a story about a dog and an elephant who both got pregnant around the same time. Fast-forward eighteen months, and the dog has given birth three times to a dozen puppies while the elephant had still not given birth from its initial pregnancy. The dog questioned whether or not the elephant was truly pregnant. The elephant's response is what struck me. She says, "What I'm growing is not what you are growing. Therefore, my timing is not your timing." This hit me for two reasons: first, the elephant knew herself. And second, she trusted her process.

Conception and birth are not on the same day for a reason. It takes time for a baby to develop in the mother's womb and it takes time for the mother's body to adjust to be able to provide and sustain the baby's life once it is birthed. Part of that adjustment process may include morning sickness, exhaustion, discomfort, and pain. It makes it easier (read: more tolerable) because the mother knows that at the end of the gestation period, a baby will be born.

The problem with patience is that we cannot always see what is being produced, or how we are developing, and we do not know how long our "gestation" period is. This is exacerbated by what we see on social media, from people whose timing is not our own.

In the summer of 2012, my high school friends and I rallied at my buddy Drew's family cabin for a few days of camping and quality time together. We were three years removed from high school, yet we still enjoyed spending time together when we could. My buddy Drew loved soccer and had played his entire life. It was time for the soccer World Cup and we watched many matches in between hiking and enjoying nature.

I view life like a World Cup soccer match. There are teams that are expert passers and have practiced sets they implement to score a goal. To the inexperienced onlooker, the passes may seem ill-advised, boring, or in the wrong direction. Admittedly, this used to be me as a child and teenager. I would watch for twenty minutes and "nothing" would be happening. Then bored, I would walk to the kitchen for a snack. Suddenly I would hear, "GOOOOOOAAAAAALLL!" coming from the TV and would sprint back just in time to see the replay.

As I grew older and began to understand the way the game is played, I learned to appreciate the seemingly mundane moments and anticipate how the passes would connect for the goal to be scored. I began to realize not every pass will be forward – not every pass can be forward – but the goal remains the same. Some games there are five goals, some games there are zero goals; some games there's a winner and a loser, and other games the teams end up tied. I have come to conclude soccer is a sport that requires resilience, patience, and consistent focused action. (We will leave the exaggerated falls alone for this metaphor.)

Soccer players do not stop playing because the match may end with zero points. They do not stop playing because 90 minutes is too long. There are times when they are sprinting, there are times when they are jogging, and there are times when they are walking. The professionals understand they must be actively engaged from the first minute through stoppage time. And while they push themselves to exhaustion, they understand that to be truly effective, they must be intentional about when and how they use their energy, lest they need to be substituted before halftime. While my experience playing soccer is limited to elementary school recess, backyard sessions, and collegiate intramurals, I have grown to love soccer because I see so many life lessons in soccer.

Patience is not sitting on the sidelines, watching the match be played or watching the marathon be run. Patience is knowing yourself and understanding that you cannot cover 26.2 miles in one second, but if you put one foot in front of the other consistently, you can reach the goal of completing a marathon. Patience is more than this. Patience is preparing for the marathon by running shorter distances of three miles, five miles, ten miles, fifteen miles, in the months leading up to the actual event in order to build the strength and endurance you need to complete the marathon.

Process reveals potential. And the process prepares you to pursue your potential. The process takes patience. Living with Enduring Urgency is living with and building your active patience.

TIME AND TIMING

Time necessitates patience. If we could set a goal and achieve it in the same second, it would reduce the value of that goal. If we could plant a seed and eat the fruit the same day, we wouldn't appreciate the fruit we ate nearly as much. The nature of a goal is defined by what we must do AND the length of time it will take us to do it.

The strategy of Enduring Urgency enables us to see time as an asset as opposed to a roadblock. The hare mentality regarding time is "I must have it now" (read: impatience) and "Ooh, what's that?" (read: distraction). The tortoise mentality views time as an asset. By making improvements (even incremental ones) each day, we can build momentum in pursuit of our goals. We will discuss this more in the next section, *Consistent Focused Action*.

This idea of delayed gratification is one that we understand regarding money, and should apply to time and goals.

While working on my financial awareness and trying to increase my financial fitness, I saw charts about what investing $1,000 at the age of 18 was valued at once the person turned 25. I felt sick thinking about the amount of money I could have had if I had invested $1,000 at 18. I quickly remembered I did not actually have $1,000 to invest at that time.

As I have reduced and eliminated my school loan debt, I have invested in various ventures. I would have loved to have been in on the initial wave of cryptocurrency investing a few years ago. But again, I was not in the right financial mindset and did not understand the time value of money.

The best time to invest in yourself was ten years ago. The best time to plant the tree was ten years ago. The next best time is today.

Know yourself.
Love yourself.
And trust <u>your</u> process.

COMPLACENCY AND CONTENTMENT

If you read only one section of this book, let it be this one. The opposite of Enduring Urgency is complacency and apathy. Complacency is defined as *"a feeling of smug or uncritical satisfaction with oneself or one's achievements."*[15] Complacency manifests itself in a variety of ways: laziness, procrastination, inaction. We feel we have lots of time, so we procrastinate on a project. We feel as though we are doing decent in our health and wellness, so we choose not to eat properly and exercise consistently. We feel things are okay in our community, so we choose not to get involved and work to improve it. At the heart of complacency is *uncritical* satisfaction; meaning that our analysis of the situation is inaccurate or incomplete. Simply put, if you are not setting goals and improving, you are losing. You are complacent. As we will discuss with our definition of success, we must be deliberately pursuing a goal. It is time to stop settling for uncritical satisfaction and convenience of ease.

Part of the internal struggle I have faced over the last few years is remaining content with life, and at the same time avoiding complacency.

So how do you remain content without becoming complacent? Therein lies what I believe to be a secret of life. I do not think it is a point you reach and then never have to worry about it again. Rather, to me it is more of a spectrum. I believe contentment is a habit built up over time by being grateful for what you have, at peace with what you don't have, and generous with what you do have. Staying content while avoiding complacency comes down to doing, and understanding how what you are doing fits into your purpose.

The following quote from Dr. Dharius Daniels is how I maintain contentment and avoid complacency.

*"How are you faithfully stewarding where you are and what you have, now? If you **do** what you're supposed to **do** in this season, and you **do** what you're supposed to **do** in the next season, and you **do** what you're supposed to **do** in the next season, you automatically and organically accomplish purpose."*[16]

The key to contentment without falling into complacency is to "do". That word is stated six times in the preceding quote because it is that important. We will discuss consistent focused action in the next section, but this needs to be said now. Patience is not passive, it is active. Patience requires action.

This quote is a reminder to be content where you are, and to make sure you are doing what you know you should be doing to keep improving and pursuing your goals and your purpose. It is a checkpoint that asks: Are you doing good when you can, where you are, with what you have? Recall the definition of urgency: Are you taking the swift action each day in service of that important thing?

This quote keeps me focused, moving forward, and trusting in the process. It keeps me content but not complacent. I hope it will do the same for you.

"How are you faithfully stewarding where you are and what you have, now? If you <u>do</u> what you're supposed to <u>do</u> in this season, and you <u>do</u> what you're supposed to <u>do</u> in the next season, and you <u>do</u> what you're supposed to <u>do</u> in the next season, you automatically and organically accomplish purpose."
– Dr. Dharius Daniels

PREPARATION

I used to have a love-hate relationship with public speaking. I thought you either were a good public speaker, or you weren't. Over time I realized this was not the case. Public speaking – like so many other "scary things" – comes down to preparation. When I am truly prepared for a briefing, a presentation, or a test, the nerves decrease or evaporate completely. I know the information so well I am more excited about getting the information across than I am concerned about my comfort "on stage".

Sometimes nerves occur because of the grandness of the stage on which you are performing. But many times, our nerves occur because we are not truly prepared for the stage we are on and we are afraid we will be exposed as a fraud. Your nerves come from a lack of preparation, not because you are unworthy to be on your stage. You are worthy to be on that stage, in that room, on that call. You are worthy to be to be on that field, in that office, behind that counter. Your preparation proves your worthiness. Your preparation will inevitably determine whether or not you are ready for the next level.

Preparation does not come easy. Many times, it occurs when no one is watching. Preparation is not the flashy moment that we sometimes dream about; rather, it is all of the tiny moments that enable you to reach that "flashy" moment. I find truth in the saying, "Luck is when preparation meets opportunity". If you are not prepared when the opportunity presents itself, you may not even realize it is an opportunity; you may see it as a burden or blindly walk right on past wondering when an opportunity will finally appear. However, if you choose to see each day as an opportunity, and prepare yourself accordingly, you will be in the position to seize the right opportunities.

In 2018, Lebron James willed his team to the 2018 National Basketball Association (NBA) Finals. Many people are in awe of Lebron and love to watch him execute throughout the game and finish off opponents. Less people are as excited to watch him practice and prepare for each game. Let me rephrase that. Before he was as dominant as he is now, few people wanted to watch him prepare. I'm not just referring to the beginning of his NBA career. Go back further. Preparation tracks back to what Lebron was doing when he was sixteen, fifteen, fourteen.

Steph Curry, another NBA player, is the same way. I came across a video interview of Steph Curry when he was a young teen. In it, he stated he wanted to play in the NBA, like his dad did. Then the clip cuts to him shooting a three as a leader on the Golden State Warriors team. He achieved his goal of making it to the NBA. What that clip did not show were the countless hours Curry put in with his parents, with coaches, and when no one was around.

The point of the previous few paragraphs is this: Preparation is a major part of patience. And preparation starts now. It is what you do to prepare for your goals when no one is around that sets you apart and enables you to achieve them. To me, preparation is part of the definition of integrity. Integrity is doing the right thing even when no one is watching. Preparation is doing whatever it takes to position yourself to achieve your goal, no matter who is (or is not) watching.

Nowadays, fans arrive two or more hours early to watch Steph Curry shoot three pointers during warm up, because they have realized that preparation is what makes him great. Preparation is active patience. Without preparation, you may miss your opportunity or fail to achieve your goal. Failing to achieve a goal can be painful; failing to achieve a goal simply because you failed to prepare for it, is unacceptable. Steven Furtick, leader of Elevation Church, said it this way: "The pain of falling short is nothing compared to the shame of stopping short." And when you fail to prepare, you are preparing to fail. You are stopping short.

So, what does preparation look like in real life? Studying for the test, reviewing the changes in regulations for the meeting with your boss, editing multiple drafts of your paper prior to submitting it, watching film on your opponent, building an agenda for the meeting you're leading so you don't waste people's time, staying after practice to lift weights. Let me take it a step further. Preparation is doing each assignment to the best of your ability and asking for help long before the test. Preparation is doing the research for your dream job and building your resume, with help if needed. Preparation is reading that book and writing a report about it to clarify your thoughts about the topic, not for credit in a class but so you can accurately share the knowledge you have gained. Preparation is mentally preparing for the week ahead on Sunday and setting your weekly goals. Preparation is waking up a few minutes earlier than normal to identify your top priorities for the day. Preparation is eating well and taking care of your health. Preparation is taking a few extra seconds to gather your thoughts before responding to a client, a teacher, or an antagonist.

Preparation may seem small or insignificant now, but do not be fooled. Preparation has a compounding effect. "Luck is when preparation meets opportunity." Do not allow an opportunity to pass you by because you were not prepared. Prepare now, and be patient knowing that in time you will bear the fruits of your labor.

DATE YOURSELF

I almost removed this section but decided to leave it in because this is applicable to you whether you are single or married. As one marriage counselor put it, "Marriage does not solve your personal issues, it exposes them." As I'm not married, I have to take that on trust.

One of my favorite books is *The Alchemist*. My brother, Sam, read my copy before I did and let me know I was missing out. I felt an urgency to finish reading it, though I was not sure why. The reason soon became clear.

My girlfriend and I were doing long-distance at the time; I was in Okinawa, Japan while she was in Texas. We met and began dating while attending Texas Tech. We broke up twice during those two and a half years. The breakups were mainly due to me not knowing what I wanted and being unsure about long-distance after I graduated.

I'm going somewhere with this.

We got back together just before I moved to Japan. She came to visit me a few months later, and we had a wonderful week together. However, I had an unsettling feeling that something was not quite right.

I soon received confirmation of events which turned my world upside-down. Super Bowl Sunday that year (well, Super Bowl Monday in Okinawa), it all came out. I remember being at the house of one of the majors in my unit with my co-workers who had turned into friends. We were watching the game when I looked down at my screen to read the incoming message. I quietly excused myself to the bathroom where I struggled to regain my breath and my composure as I reread the message that meant our relationship was over. I suddenly understood the idea of heartbreak and not being able to breathe because of it.

The ensuing six months were some of the most challenging of my life. I found myself truly alone; an ocean away from family and close friends, in a country I was still learning about, in a job I had only recently begun to understand.

It was around this time that I read *The Alchemist* for the first time and it truly changed my life. I began to view life as an adventure and pay attention to how events were working together. As I stated earlier, my faith was a major factor in getting me through this period. My close friends and my family checked on me regularly. But there was no one there at night when I was struggling to fall asleep, questioning God, my existence, and my worth.

During the day, I threw myself completely into my work, learning as much as I could, trying to compartmentalize what had happened so I could progress in my young career. But there were inevitably days when I would get lost in thought while I should have been completing a task or preparing for a briefing.

As I went back through *The Alchemist*, I began to note how he was on a journey to find his personal legend and he had some major setbacks. He had a period of feeling sorry for himself. Then he changed his perspective and decided to consider his loss as part of his larger journey. I decided to do the same.

Even now when I share with people that I would (and still do) go to brunch on my own on the weekends, they look at me weird. I remember having the thought, *I have no responsibilities other than to heal and improve myself right now.* It was truly liberating. I would spend an entire day reading and researching, driving and exploring the beautiful island, thinking and praying.

During this time, I was able to envision what I wanted my life to look like, who I wanted to be, and what I wanted to do. I had a blank canvas, and it was up to me to faithfully steward what was and what would become my life.

While I did not have the phrase at that time, I understood and was living with Enduring Urgency. I knew healing would be difficult and take time, and I knew I would have to take consistent focused action to accomplish the vision and goals I had for my life. I understood I could no longer delay my healing and that only through acknowledging the pain I was in, would I be able to move forward with my life and pursue my purpose, which was becoming clearer by the day.

I went through a difficult time with that break-up and I would not wish that on anyone. But looking back, I can say I am truly thankful for it because of the experiences I had afterwards as I was finding myself and discovering who I wanted to be. It was a difficult yet empowering time.

As I stated before, the reason we broke up the first two times was because I was not sure of what I wanted and thus I was unsure if I wanted to do long-distance after graduating. It is difficult to know what you want when you do not know who you are. It is difficult to know what to search for if you do not know what you need. It is difficult to ask for what you do not know you need. In learning about yourself, you begin to understand who you want to be, what you want in life, what you need in a friend, in a partner, in your life.

In hindsight, I know I did not fully know myself during college and while I was in that relationship. I did both myself and my girlfriend a disservice by dating her before I had dated myself.

At the risk of overstepping, I have seen relationships fail because one or both people did not truly know themselves before getting into the relationship. Or, one person was able to find themselves during the relationship and realized that partner was not who they needed.

I believe dating yourself is part of learning and developing patience.

Below are a couple of the exercises I did during this self-discovery process. I am a firm believer in principles along with tangible tools to implement those principles into your life.

1.)   *What I Love, What I Want, What I Fear*

For these first three, I literally took a blank sheet of notebook paper, wrote each title and spent the next hour thinking and writing honestly. This process enabled me to be transparent with myself and helped clarify what was important to me, what truly mattered.

2.)   *Myself in 10 Years*

Around that time, I came across an acceptance speech that Matthew McConaughey gave. In it he says, *"The person I chase is me in ten years. Every day, every week, every month, and every year of my life, my hero is always 10 years away. I am never gonna be my hero... and that's just fine with me because it keeps me with somebody to keep on chasing."*[17] I believe this idea fits perfectly with the idea of constantly learning, growing, and improving because you want to be your best self. I needed to find out what "me in ten years" looks like. It was my way of adding teeth to my vision and turning my dreams into actionable goals.

What do you look like in 10 years?

IN A WORLD OF
POTATOES
AND EGGS,
BE COFFEE.

WHEN BOILED, POTATOES GET SOFT AND EGGS BECOME
HARD. WHEN COFFEE GROUNDS MEET BOILING WATER, THEY
INFUSE THEIR FLAVOR INTO THE WATER AND TURN IT INTO
COFFEE. COFFEE CHANGES THE WATER, RATHER THAN
ALLOW THE WATER TO CHANGE IT.

EDUCATION & LEARNING

"Education is the most powerful weapon which you can use to change the world." – Nelson Mandela[18]

I am passionate about education and learning.

Do not limit your learning to the classroom. You can learn from books, from asking questions, from researching using the internet, and from talking to people who have had different experiences than you.

Reading is crucial to your growth. I recommend reading a mixture of non-fiction and fiction books; non-fiction to gain new knowledge and fiction to expand your imagination.

The French word for learn is "apprendre", which is where we get the word apprehend. As in apprehending (or capturing) a suspect. I love this visual of having to pursue and capture new information. It is accurate. If you want to learn and subsequently grow your vocabulary and knowledge, you cannot sit back and expect to learn passively. You must be purposeful in your pursuit of learning.

And once you capture that information, do not be afraid to share what you have learned with other people. Sharing new knowledge is important for two reasons. First, by teaching someone, you reinforce that knowledge in your own mind. Second, we produce better products, companies, programs, and services when we collaborate using our diverse experiences in pursuit of a common goal. Too often this life is seen as a zero-sum game (for me to win, someone else must lose). Instead, I believe that Simon Sinek is right in saying that *Together is Better.*

Learning a new language is a great way to build both resilience and patience. At the most basic level, learning a new language enables you to communicate and connect with more people. The act of learning a new language gives insight into and empathy for people who are speaking your language as their second or third language. And the daily act of practicing the new language builds your resilience because making mistakes and being corrected are part of the process of learning a new language. Language proficiency does not happen immediately, but takes consistent focused action over time to improve.

As I learned French over the past couple years, I became increasingly impressed by people who can speak multiple languages. I used to think they had special abilities that enabled them to learn multiple languages. And it is true that some people may be better at learning languages than others. But, in viewing bilingual or multilingual people as special, I removed my urge to learn a new language and I devalued the resilience, patience, and consistent focused action of those who could speak multiple languages.

It is important to acknowledge the Enduring Urgency required to learn a new language. Often it is to better provide for one's family, to assimilate into a new place, to communicate with more people, to expand a skillset in order to be of more value to society. Whatever the reason, learning a new language is a process which requires the three tenants of Enduring Urgency, and can build up your resilience and patience.

MENTORING AND HOW TO GET IT

Ask. Sometimes it is that simple. While I was in Okinawa, I was able to meet and interact with several successful military and community leaders. One of those leaders was the Executive

Director of the Society of American Military Engineers at the time, retired Army General Joseph Schroedel.

The first time I was able to have an extended conversation with him, he shared with me his life journey, his career path, and what made him, him. I was so fascinated and encouraged by his leadership skills, faith, consistency, and selfless service, I eventually asked him if we could have a follow-up conversation in time. He graciously obliged and we had a couple hour-long phone conversations over the following months. He shared so much with me about leadership, non-profit work, and personal growth, for which I am eternally grateful. He shared one quote that I believe in wholeheartedly:

"Invest in yourself, your development, your people, your friends, your outfit. In short, never miss an opportunity to grow."

We live in an amazing age of technology where you do not have to have physical contact with someone to learn from them. As I stated in the dedication of this book, two of my mentors who are probably unaware that they are my mentors are Stephen Furtick (lead pastor of Elevation Church) and Dr. Dharius Daniels (lead pastor of Change Church). It was actually during Elevation's 2016 Code Orange Revival that I was exposed to the eloquent brilliance of Dr. Daniels. And when I found out my next assignment would be in New Jersey, I was ecstatically surprised to find out Change Church was based there.

These two gentlemen have poured into my life so much over the years, and I want to thank them for their mentorship from a distance. Through YouTube, podcasts, and their social media platforms, I am encouraged and exposed to new ideas.

Ask for mentorship if you want it. The worst that can happen is the person says no, which is completely understandable. If you are going to ask someone to be your mentor, be prepared. I love the story John Maxwell tells about meeting Coach John Wooden. The rendezvous came about by John Maxwell asking someone his patented "Who do you know that I should know?" question. Turns out, that person knew Coach Wooden and set up a meeting.

In preparation for the meeting, Mr. Maxwell read every book Coach Wooden had written, and then wrote out four pages of questions. As Mr. Maxwell explains it, Coach Wooden was both impressed and encouraged by his preparation and the quantity of questions when they met for breakfast, and Coach Wooden invited him back to his house to continue the conversation. Coach Wooden patiently poured into John Maxwell in part because John Maxwell was well-prepared and had taken action which created the opportunity.

Let me stop here: if you are going to ask someone to be your mentor, be prepared. Ensure they know you value their time and are grateful by studying and preparing ahead of time. As we discussed earlier, "luck" is when preparation meets opportunity. Do not waste your opportunity meeting someone you regard highly by not preparing to make the most of your mentorship meeting. Their time is valuable, and they are being generous with it, so you not being prepared is disrespectful.

Between books, podcasts, and video recordings, you can be mentored by and mentor people without ever coming face-to-face.

There is a hidden side of asking for help. Now that I am aware of how best to serve, I have the responsibility to incorporate the wisdom I've gained into my daily actions. I can no longer claim ignorance. I must elevate my thinking and my actions. And possibly that's why some people don't ask for help. Because once you know how to fish and have the fishing rod, you are responsible for whether you (and your team) eat.

I am a result of the generous people who have taken the time to pour into me over the years. My goal is to make sure their generosity does not go to waste. To maximize their generosity by paying it forward. This book is one way I am trying to pay it forward.

Who are some of your mentors? What have you learned from them? Use the page to reflect.

NOTES

The greatest ideas
and intentions mean nothing
if you do not
ACT ON THEM.

SECTION III: CONSISTENT FOCUSED ACTION

Action (noun): the fact or process of doing something, typically to achieve <u>an aim</u>[19]
Focused (adj): with your attention directed to what you want to do; with <u>very clear aims</u>[20]
Consistent (adj): marked by harmony, regularity, or steady continuity: free from variation or contradiction[21]

There comes a point when you need to act. And that time is now. Urgency is *Importance requiring swift action.* Your life is important. Your family is important. Your community is important. And that importance requires you to act. Now. Simply talking about or planning something is not enough.

This section excites me because when you act consistently, you can turn your knowledge into know-how. It is in doing that we learn and grow.

There have been times I planned to do something, or wanted to do something, but delayed doing it because I wanted to think it through. In truth, "thinking it through" was really me not believing I could do it, me feeling unqualified to do it, or me being afraid of failure and what people would say. Do your due diligence, use what you have, prepare yourself, and then do it. Understand you may make mistakes. That is okay.

I have been self-conscious about my teeth since elementary school; I never had braces and my teeth weren't horrible, but I was self-conscious. For a while as an adult I wanted braces, then my mind changed when I heard J. Cole's verse in *Crooked Smile* where he says, "I keep my twisted grill, just to show them kids it's real". I felt those lyrics and wanted to put my imperfections to good use and show people that you do not have to be perfect to make an impact. So, I waited.

As with other areas of my life, I decided to take the necessary action to improve my teeth, and ultimately my smile. Around the beginning of 2019, I decided to research and ultimately invest in teeth aligners. After reading some legal documents, signing them, and reviewing the cost, I went into a room with an associate who gave me some additional information. She then told me that she needed to take pictures of my teeth to make an accurate assessment of my mouth and what would need to be done. She told me this photographing part would be uncomfortable, but was part of the process.

The camera takes about 6,000 photos each second to create a three-dimensional model of your mouth. About three weeks later, a purple box arrived with all of the aligners I would need for the duration of the process. In total, there were 18 aligners spread out over 168 days. As I opened the box and began reading the instructions, I began to smile. This company created a profile of my mouth and laid out a plan to align my teeth and brighten my smile.

The instructions informed me that each of the aligners was labeled so I would know exactly when to put each one in. Further, I was to take pictures of my mouth to document the changes, and I would speak with a dentist periodically. Once I input my information on their website, I saw the countdown which showed how much longer I had to go to my "ideal smile".

I hope you can see where I am going with this.

The company gave me everything I needed to align my teeth, and the 18 different plastic aligners were created to provide incremental adjustments to my teeth. Just as we don't know our "gestation" period (see the *Patience* Section), most of the time in life, we are unable to see exactly what the end result of our consistent focused action will be, nor do we have a step-by-step plan developed for us to follow. Though they gave me a sleek purple box with everything I needed in it, my teeth would not have become aligned if I did not utilize each of the aligners in the timing and manner instructed (anytime I was not eating, after brushing, and flossing my teeth). It would not have worked if I did not act.

Similarly, the plan would not have work if I tried to skip to the fifth aligner on Day 1. There would have been a lot of pain and the aligners may not have fit because that set was for my mouth at a later stage. This was where patience came into play. Just as the process of realigning my teeth took time and consistently using the aligners, your life is a process of intentionally taking consistent actions that over time will produce your desired result.

The instructions also warned to expect some discomfort. Each aligner was pushing my teeth in a direction they were not used to, but would ultimately be my desired outcome. Consequently, the aligners were not comfortable when they were in and my teeth were sensitive when I took the aligners out. This was where resilience came in. Consistent focused action will not always be comfortable. You may be changing a habit that you have had for decades. And just like my teeth, those habits have deep roots. Your progress will not come without a cost. In my case, the cost was money and comfort. In your case, the cost may be one of those, both, or something else entirely. A loss of comfort is inevitable if you are changing a habit. And that is okay. Your progress is worth more than your comfort. Get comfortable being uncomfortable.

THE COMPOUNDING EFFECT

The reason for consistent focused action is the compounding effect – the large and long-term consequences of a series of small choices. I came across the book *The Compound Effect* by Darren Hardy towards the end of writing this book. I was in Barnes & Noble with my best friend Shamel, and the moment I saw the title, it clicked.

According to Hardy, the compound effect is the principle of reaping huge rewards from a series of small, smart choices. And just like gravity, this law does not care who you are. You can benefit greatly from taking consistent focused action, or you can suffer the consequences of idleness, inaction, and distraction.

Enduring Urgency is about building up your resilience and patience through consistent focused action and in order to take consistent focused action. It is a mindset and process that builds as it is implemented. This section is about doing, doing consistently, and hurdles to be aware of as you do. Let's do it!

SUCCESS REDEFINED

In thinking about Enduring Urgency, it was apparent that I needed to redefine success for myself.

As I was writing this book, I came across a speech by Earl Nightingale by way of Dave Ramsey. In listening to it, Earl Nightingale recited a definition of success that I have adopted as my own. If it helps, insert your name and your pronoun where appropriate.

"Success is the progressive realization of a worthy ideal. If a man is working towards a predetermined goal and knows where he is going, that man is a success. If he is not doing that, he is a failure... A success is anyone who is doing deliberately a predetermined job because that is what he decided to do."[22]

Put another way, identifying a goal and actively working towards it makes you successful. Taking consistent focused action for our important thing is the embodiment of success. This definition allows us to enjoy the process of pursuing a goal instead of waiting until the end of a goal to determine if we have been successful. I am successful *because* I am pursuing my goals. As I am taking consistent focused action, momentum is building and is propelling me towards my goals.

Earl Nightingale's definition of success holds the three keys of Enduring Urgency: resilience, patience, and consistent focused action. "...progressive realization of a worthy ideal" lets us know obtaining a goal happens over time, so we must practice patience.

"…Working towards a predetermined goal" captures the idea of consistent focused action. The underlying theme is resilience; that in the progressive realization of a worthy ideal, you may have some setbacks, and that is okay, so long as you deliberately keep doing a predetermined job because that is what you decided to do.

I offer this definition of success for you to internalize in your own life and in the pursuit of your goals. I believe that this definition sets a solid framework for taking consistent focused action in the pursuit of your goals and purpose.

"I have observed that
setting a goal makes no appeal
to the mediocre. But to those fired with
an ambition really to achieve greatly,
setting a goal becomes a program
that stirs the inner soul to action."
– William Danforth[23]

PRIORITIES

Prioritizing your time and thus your action is all about intentionality. At work, I used to make a list of the things I wanted to get done by the end of the day and then check them off as I accomplished each task. Somehow, by the end of the day, my list had grown, even though I crossed some things off.

I created a tool to better suit my life and my process. The definition of urgency is *"importance requiring swift action"*. Within the definition of urgent is the word important. Therefore, one category is *Urgent* (important and requiring swift action); the second is *Important* (important but not requiring swift action); the third is *Distractions* (not important, may seem like it requires swift action).

"Urgent" – These items get your attention first. Priority one items. These items should be directly tied to your weekly goals, your work responsibilities, your life's purpose.

"Important" – This is the second priority section. These items are just as important, but there may not be an immediate deadline to completing them; they do not require swift action. If you wait too long to address these items, they may become "Urgent" in a negative way. If you don't make time for your health, you will eventually have to make time for it when you get sick. If you do not make time for your family, you may wake up one day and realize that those relationships are there in name only, and you no longer have those authentic connections.

"Distractions" – These items may feel important in the moment because they have a time component, but they do not help me accomplish my goals. Distractions can be reevaluated periodically.

Sometimes, we allow the "Distractions" to supersede the "Urgent" and "Important" in our daily actions. The result for me when I make this mistake is that I get to the end of the day feeling drained from putting out a lot of fires, but I do not feel as though I have made real progress in the things that matter. It is important to write down all items and then to categorize them in order to ensure that your efforts are focused on the urgent and the important, rather than the distractions.

De-plating is an effective tool to dealing with distractions. Imagine you are eating something delicious and you want more of it but you also have something on your plate that you don't like as much. By leaving the undesirable substance on your plate, you take up space that could be holding more of the deliciousness.

De-plating is the concept of actually removing an item from your proverbial plate so you no longer think about it and you can focus on those urgent and important things. This is challenging because these may be fun things or easier activities. It may be an event or even a person that you may have known for a long time.

The larger piece to this is identifying what is important to you, what you believe your purpose is, and writing out your life vision and mission statements. From there, you can take purposeful action as you align your weekly goals with your monthly goals, your monthly goals to your annual goals, your annual goals to your future self.

I reduced hours of effort to the single preceding paragraph. I want you to know this process will take time. It will take intentionality. And it will take consistency. Which is why the first two parts of this Enduring Urgency strategy are resilience and patience. The preceding paragraph occurred as part of my self-discovery process and the "Loves", "Wants", "Fears" lists I discussed in the *Patience* Section.

I want to return to a question I posed earlier. What is important to you? Use the next page to answer this question.

What is important to you?

Do

"Physical strength demands exercise. Mental alertness demands study. Winsome personality thrives on service. Religious growth requires action, the actual doing of right things instead of the wrong. We advance only by doing."
— William Danforth[24]

It is tough to say it more succinctly than Mr. Danforth. We advance, we improve, we build only by doing. Endurance is built only by doing something repeatedly. We build endurance in running by pushing ourselves to exhaustion, which establishes a new baseline of capacity to endure for our mind and body. The same for action: there will days when you are exhausted, and you see no progress. Take heart. Your endurance is building.

The definition of urgency has within it *swift action*; doing swiftly. The Enduring Urgency strategy is worthless for you if you do not put it to work.

Action speaks louder than words and our lives speak louder than any powerful quote or bible verse. Building resilience requires effort. Developing patience – active patience – requires effort. Taking consistent focused action requires effort. Employing the Enduring Urgency strategy requires effort.

I DARE YOU to DO the work required to build yourself up and improve yourself, and DO the work required to build your community.

Consistency

Consistency (noun): The quality or fact of staying the same at different times[25]

Consistency (noun): The quality or fact of having parts that agree with each other[26]

Consistency is one of the most undervalued words and is at the heart of Enduring Urgency. The urgency is consistent for an extended period; the course of one's life. I didn't initially realize how important consistency was, but after learning French for my advising job, I realized that Focused Action is not good enough on its own. You must take *consistent* focused action.

So, EU = R + P + CFA = Success.

Consistency really speaks to being disciplined. While writing this book, the following quote was the lock-screen on my phone: "You won't always be motivated. That's why you have to learn to be disciplined." Jim Collins explains this as the Flywheel Effect. Imagine pushing a large wheel. If you apply constant force in a specific direction, the wheel will continue moving in the desired direction. It will be difficult to get it moving at first due to friction, but in time it will move. It takes consistent focused action to build the momentum of the flywheel. If you act sporadically it takes much more time and energy to get the wheel up to speed, if you ever do.

Focused action is important, but the phrase does not get to the root of the issue of the hare. He was swift, but he was beaten by Slow and Steady. It wasn't the slow part that enabled the tortoise to defeat the hare. Rather it was that the tortoise was moving forward, and was *steady* in his movement; he was consistent while the hare was swift but sporadic.

In the race of swift and sporadic versus slow and sporadic, swift and sporadic wins. In the race of swift and sporadic versus slow and steady, the latter is victorious. In this case, it does not appear that the tortoise was slow by today's definition; it was a race and he exhibited a sense of urgency in his movement. While he may have been slower than the hare, he was moving at his own speed, which, together with his consistency, allowed him to win the race. The tortoise was deliberate throughout the race. As we continue to apply the principles of resilience, patience, and consistent focused action to our daily lives, we establish the foundation of Enduring Urgency and build momentum. Before you know it, you are operating at a swift and steady pace.

I absolutely love the word *consistency*. It has two meanings; the first speaks to being steady in one's actions. The other speaks to what a substance is made of. And I could not think of a better word to have such a dual meaning. What are you made of? What are we made of? Writer Will Durant (not Aristotle) once eloquently articulated, "We are what we repeatedly do. Excellence, then, is not an act, but a habit." Our consistency (read: our habits, what we repeatedly do) creates our consistency (read: who we are). As Mr. Durant pointed out, we can tell a lot about a person by their habits. Who we are is shaped by what we repeatedly do. We create our habits, and our habits in turn define who we are. Therein lies the power and necessity of consistent focused action.

I purposefully did not include a piece titled "Balance". While I understand the sentiment, I do not believe balance is the right word to capture how the different areas of your life best intertwine. I believe harmony is the better word. You should strive for harmony in your actions and in your life. In fact, consistency includes the concept of harmony. As you continue to take consistent focused action in pursuit of your goals, you improve yourself and increase the harmony of your life.

Consistency speaks to
being disciplined in your actions.
You will not always be motivated.
That's why
You must be disciplined.

DISTRACTION, DISTR-ACTION, DIS-TRACTION

With action, comes distractions. When working on this project, I have enjoyed looking up the definitions of the key words I am using because the current use of the word does not always line up with the original definition.

The word *distraction* originates from the Latin distrahere, literally to draw apart. Not draw, in the artistic sense. But draw as in "drawn and quartered"[27].

When I think about the word distraction, I like this visual of being pulled away from my purpose, pulled away from my priorities, pulled away from what matters to me most. And while your typical distraction causes no physical pain, I view distraction as ripping me and my purpose apart.

As I have begun viewing distractions like this, it has helped me reduce my susceptibility to them, in their many varieties. I'd be lying if I said I didn't get distracted, but my goal is to take consistent focused action.

In the Disney animation of the tortoise and the hare, the hare is feeding off the crowd prior to the race starting and eventually gets distracted by a few pretty members of the crowd during the race. This is the perfect place to say this: do not allow the crowd (or lack thereof) to distract you from pursuing your goal. DO NOT LET THE CROWD, OR LACK THEREOF, DISTRACT YOU FROM YOUR GOAL.

The tortoise could have chosen to be discouraged and not participate because no one was cheering for him. Instead, he went about his business. For us, we may not have a physical crowd; in our age, it may appear as laughs in a classroom or likes on a post.

I must admit I am guilty of playing to the crowd at times. I share a thought and am enamored by the number of people who agree with or appreciate what I am doing. Or conversely, I feel disappointed if I share a tool I find useful and only a few people acknowledge the tool's utility or my act. It is in those moments I remind myself of the tortoise, and how he ran his race without being concerned about what the crowd was saying and doing. Now that I know my purpose (to serve God by loving people and uniting them), my life is more about being obedient to God and living in integrity, and less about what people think. I am human, so this crowd distraction is one I must be vigilant against.

I began with priorities for a reason. To understand distractions and your susceptibility to them, you must first understand your priorities. That way you can take consistent focused action. Anything outside of that *focused* action can be a distraction. Only once you have identified where you will focus your action (rewrite: Only once you have focused your action) will you be able to identify what is a distraction versus what are your responsibilities and priorities.

When you allow yourself to become distracted, you lose traction and momentum on what you are working on. It's part of Jim Collins' Flywheel Effect I mentioned in *"Consistency"*. You may get the wheel moving but if you stop applying constant force to look at or do something else, that wheel will eventually come to a stop. You will have to start again with the process of getting the wheel moving.

The same principle is true of consistent focused action and distractions. Distractions cause dis-traction, a loss of traction and momentum in the work you are doing. I've noticed this in my social media presence. When I am posting weekly, the momentum begins to build, and I *feel* that I am helping more people as they come to expect a new post from me. However, when I go for an extended period without posting, that internal momentum and any external momentum that was building seems to reset.

Distractions are the antithesis of consistent focused action. This means you must be VIGILANT (read: diligent, defensive, deliberate) with your time and energy. That doesn't prevent you from being generous with your time and being willing to change your plans to help someone. It simply means tell your time and energy and focus where to go, or you will wonder where they went. It may be as simple as building in some time for unexpected opportunities to help someone. Or for social media or a book or your favorite TV show, if that is your way of relaxing.

This comes back to knowing yourself, loving yourself, and trusting your process. Knowing yourself enough to identify what is part of your relaxation process versus what is you simply wasting time. Loving yourself enough to take time for physical, emotional, and spiritual health and wellness. And trusting that if you truly put forth your best effort over time, constantly strive to improve, and use your life to serve others (be it the immediate people around you or your future descendants), you will live a full, purpose-filled life.

INACTION

In talking about action, I reflected on inaction and the cost of inaction. Yes, there is a cost to inaction. Investors and day-traders understand this, but it seems to be lost in the daily grind. I received a rough reminder of this important truth that has stuck with me over time.

There is a cost to inaction. The cost is missed opportunity. It is easy to see the cost of a missed opportunity when you are dealing with dollars and cents. This cost is more difficult to see when you are dealing with plans you did not follow through on, projects you never completed, thoughts you never shared, or passions that you never pursued.

And here's where I reveal a bit of myself: Inaction frustrates me. I can tell when I haven't been doing what I believe I am supposed to do because I am in a frustrated mood.

Inaction frustrates me because internally I understand that inaction leads to missed opportunities and not walking in my full potential. Yet, I rarely see tangible consequences from my inaction. Back in 2017, it was different. At the time, I became increasingly aware of the potential of cryptocurrency, then researched blockchains and some of the coins, such as Bitcoin, Ripple, and Ethereum. After a few months of learning I had an opportunity to buy a coin before I thought it would take off.

This is similar to buying a stock before the price increases. I decided not to buy but continued to watch this coin's trajectory over the next few days. As I anticipated, the coin significantly increased in value. Had I seized this opportunity, it would have been a substantial monetary win.

My initial reaction was one of frustration with myself, and regret. After a few minutes (and a quick venting session with my buddy), I determined to use the skills and abilities which put me in the position for the previous opportunity to prepare for the next opportunity, and I focused on ensuring the same mistake would not be not repeated.

I believe it is beneficial to see a tangible opportunity lost as a real-world lesson of the opportunities we may lose if we do not act. In other words, seeing a missed opportunity can be the kick we need to act. That said, I won't be needing another one of these lessons again; this one will stick. In fact, I printed a copy of the missed opportunity – a chart of the coin's trajectory – as a daily reminder to passionately pursue my purpose lest I not experience the full potential of God's plan for my life.

Often, we have intentions of calling someone, or helping someone, or writing that book, or completing that project. Yet, we put it off, not realizing we may have missed an opportunity by procrastinating. Someone once said, "the opportunity of a lifetime must be seized in the lifetime of the opportunity." I believe this wholeheartedly. The problem comes because we cannot always physically see what we are giving up because of our inaction. I say "giving up" because inaction is a choice, so by not acting, we are choosing to give up an opportunity.

That opportunity may be as simple as making someone smile, improving someone's day, exposing someone to new ideas, or encouraging someone to pursue their own purpose.

Inaction on intentions lead to missed opportunities. Inaction has a cost. Do not allow your inaction to forfeit your future.

My mantra for the 2018 was "Focused Action" and "Use Every Arrow". (Thank you, Pastor Furtick!) The first is a reminder to prioritize and stay focused on my purpose and ensure my actions are aligned with my goals, and my goals are aligned with my purpose. The second part is a reminder to use every talent, idea, and opportunity I have been blessed with in line with my purpose. Leave no arrow unused.

I DARE YOU to develop yourself, follow through on your plans, complete your projects, share your thoughts, pursue your passions. Walk in your purpose. And do not delay; there is a cost to your inaction.

INTEGRITY REVISITED

Integrity is not perfection; it's authenticity and a spirit of excellence. This idea is so important I want to address it twice. Steph Curry does not stop shooting three-pointers because he goes 2 for 11 in the first half. He continues shooting, figures out what he needs to do to correct his shot, and gets back on fire. It comes down to resilience: the capacity to recover quickly from difficulties. The capacity to recover quickly enough that when you come down the basketball court 30 seconds after missing a three-point attempt, you're ready to fire up another one, regardless of who's guarding you. The capacity to recover quickly from a wrong answer in class and be ready and willing to answer the next question that comes your way. The capacity to recover quickly from making an error at work and be ready to take on the next assignment with energy and focus.

Integrity is not perfection; it's excellent authenticity. I will always do my best when taking consistent focused action. And if I make a mistake, I refuse to hide and not take on another challenge. I call mistakes life lessons. I will learn from that lesson and implement the newfound wisdom into my next action.

Let's review the definition of success you read earlier: *"Success is the progressive realization of a worthy ideal. If a man is working towards a predetermined goal and knows where he is going, that man is a success. If he is not doing that, he is a failure… A success is anyone who is doing deliberately a predetermined job because that is what he decided to do."*

My definition of success is not tied to the result of a specific goal; rather, I am successful so long as I am taking purposeful action towards the achievement of my goal. I am no longer bound to external forces for my ultimate success.

If my goal is to improve the culture of my team and increase the effectiveness of my team, then I am successful as I am working on the teambuilding activities it takes to create a great culture, and implementing the tools to increase the effectiveness. Now, if we win team of the quarter or team of the year, we are simply being acknowledged for our effectiveness and the service we delivered to our unit.

If my goal as a parent is to raise a daughter who is thoughtful, caring, hard-working and a productive member of society, I do not have to wait until she turns 18 to know if I have done a good job. I am successful while I am raising her so long as I am deliberately doing the job of being her father. It is my responsibility to provide for her and raise her to be thoughtful, caring, hard-working, and a productive member of society. At a certain point she will make her own decisions and she will be responsible for her own success. And if I make a mistake as a father and miss a soccer match, I have NOT failed as a parent. It simply means that if one of my goals is to never miss a match, then I did not meet that specific goal.

Warning: Do not use making a mistake or not achieving a specific goal as an excuse to stop trying. And I urge you: DO NOT allow one error to disrupt your momentum and dismantle your progress.

In learning the French language over the past year, I would use the language application Duolingo. There was a week when I set a goal of seven days in a row, and after completing Days One through Four, I forgot and missed Day Five. I remembered on Day Six, realized my streak was broken, and allowed a single lost day to turn into a week of inaction on that application. I put more focus on the one missed day rather than celebrate the fact that I completed language training on Duolingo for five out of six days. I have had to work on celebrating small victories instead of going into a slump because of a mistake or failure.

Integrity is not perfection; it is excellent authenticity. You may make mistakes in the pursuit of your goal, but the simple fact that you have identified a goal and are actively working towards it makes you successful. This new perspective on success does not excuse us from being responsible for our lives, working to improve ourselves, and positively impacting our sphere of influence. This perspective equips and encourages us to operate in success because we are taking consistent focused action to accomplish our goals; we are striving to live in our purpose by living on purpose.

Read this as many times
as you need to:

Do not use making a mistake or
failing to achieve a specific goal
as an excuse to stop trying.
Do not allow one error to
disrupt your momentum and
dismantle your progress.

INTENTIONALITY

Live on purpose. You must be intentional about what you choose to focus on. You must be intentional about the actions you take. You must be intentional to be consistent.

Consistent Focused Action is a choice. Enduring Urgency is a choice. You must choose to see your life as larger than you; if you are a parent, you have a leg up on seeing the world through legacy lenses. There is a drive to provide for and create opportunities for your child to succeed. If you are not married, that's okay. At the time of this writing I'm not married.

As I stated in "Date Yourself", I chase myself in ten years. I heard Matthew McConaughey say this in an award speech a few years ago and it resonated with me. Once again, he said, *"Every day, every week, every month, and every year of my life, my hero is always 10 years away. I am never gonna be my hero... and that's just fine with me because it keeps me with somebody to keep on chasing."* I have since adopted this idea as I believe it fits perfectly with the idea of constantly learning, growing, doing, and improving because you want to be your best self. For a while I simply said it. Then I decided to identify the attributes, certifications, skills, accomplishments I want in thirty-seven-year-old me. This task was not simple, but it was fun because I essentially wrote down who I want to be and what I want to have done and be doing ten years from that day. I then was able to reverse-engineer to this current year and identify what specifically I need to be doing each day to catch the snapshot of myself in ten years.

GRATITUDE

This idea could have gone in the *Resilience* Section. Being grateful builds resilience. Expressing gratitude means taking consistent focused action to demonstrate your awareness of the blessings in your life.

I started *The People We Meet* writing project to highlight those people who have had an impact on my life. Too often we wait until someone's funeral to express their impact on our lives. I wanted to change that. By acknowledging the impact of others on your life, you set yourself up to be blessed by other people because they know you will be grateful and you will maximize what you have been given. The last part of the previous sentence is key. You should not express gratitude to receive more. You should express gratitude because you have received so much already.

As I've understood how much I have to be grateful for, it has encouraged me to make the most of every opportunity and to help as many people as possible because there are many people who do not have access to the same opportunities I have. I must be a conduit of the generosity and resources bestowed to me.

Some people make the mistake of denying that they started out in a better position or had more opportunities than others. It is in the act of denying those shoulders we stand on, that we limit our gratitude and undermine our purpose.

Gratitude reciprocates. Gratitude takes purposeful action and enables me to take purposeful action.

About a year ago, I began keeping a jar in my kitchen along with small notecards. At the end of the day, I would reflect and write down one thing I was grateful for that day. This helped me take stock of all the people, opportunities, and experiences in my life.

I Dare You to do this each day for 27 days. Why 27? Because it's three times nine. It's an odd number, which will hopefully help you remember.

FOOD

What have you eaten today? On the surface, this may seem like an odd question to ask. But I want you to take fifteen seconds to think about exactly what you have consumed in the past 24 hours. Now, I imagine you are thinking about what you had for breakfast, lunch, and dinner. I am.

More than referring to what you have put in your body, I am referring to what you have put in your mind and spirit. What have you eaten (read: listened to, watched, read) over the past 24 hours? You may need more than fifteen seconds to remember everything. Just as the food we eat affects us physically, the "food" we eat can affect us mentally, emotionally, and spiritually. What we eat may seem inconsequential but has a massive impact on us in the short and long term.

In Okinawa, my friend Jon decided to participate in a Physique Competition. I saw firsthand the resilience, patience, and consistent focused action he put forth in the months leading up to the competition. He was successful because he set a goal and worked to accomplish it. In talking to him, the hardest part was not going to work out each day; he enjoyed most of the workouts. The biggest challenge for him was eating the right food at the right time. He would meal prep every weekend with his wife, Kalesia. She would sometimes eat what he was eating, but most of the time his meals were too "boring". He would eat essentially the same meals at the same time each day so that he would have the required energy when he needed it at the gym and so that he could burn as much fat as possible. It was great to be there with him throughout his process. In transparency, some days he was more motivated than others. Some days he wanted to eat a cheeseburger instead of his grilled chicken and vegetables. But he stuck with the program. He would have his occasional cheat meal as planned, then would be back to the programmed meals. Jon ended up winning the island-wide Physique Competition and we celebrated by eating delicious cheeseburgers at a local restaurant.

I've had multiple friends train for physique competitions and what strikes me is not necessarily their consistency in the gym, but their commitment and consistency to the meal plan. We often focus on our output – actions, words – yet fail to take note of what we are putting into or allowing into our minds.

Eating two cookies in a day may seem inconsequential, but if you eat two chewy chocolate chip cookies every day for 365 days, you will undoubtedly feel (and see) the results. At best, it will slow your progress down. At worst, it will affect your energy, weight, and health over time.

What you feed yourself will affect you physically, mentally, emotionally, and spiritually. An easy way to take stock of your mood and what you are consuming is to write down everything you literally eat and everything you figuratively eat for a 24-hour period. Then review it and see if all that food is moving you towards your goals or away from your goals.

Stop...
WHAT ARE YOU EATING?
And how is it affecting you?

PRAY

Just as I initially had hesitations about including the chapter *"Faith, Facts, and God"*, I hesitated to include this topic. But again, if I did not include it, I would not be providing you with a complete formula and thus would be doing you a disservice.

I used to think prayer was all about what we said. I'm learning that praying is often more about listening. Quiet time is about focusing your thoughts and planning your actions before the chaos of the day begins. As you consistently give your mind time to focus, the things that matter will come to the forefront. This is winning.

When I was living in Washington, D.C. in 2014, I visited National Community Church, led by Mark Batterson. One of the gifts I received for being a first-time guest was *The Circle Maker*, written by Pastor Batterson. This book introduces Honi the Circle Maker, and it encouraged me to pray boldly and consistently. I began giving this book to friends because it made such a big impact in my life. Prior to me leaving Okinawa, I had dinner with my buddy Jon, his wife Kalesia, and our friend Kate at Kate's place. I gave Kate a copy of *The Circle Maker*. Her eyes lit up, she walked out of the room, and walked back with a copy of *Draw the Circle*, the prayer plan to Mark Batterson's *The Circle Maker*. She gave it to me, which completely caught me off guard.

I worked through the 40-day prayer plan when I first arrived in New Jersey and it was powerful. Over the past few weeks, I picked it back up and began again as part of my morning devotion and journal time. This time is so important to me, but if I am not deliberate, I will give up my devotional time for other activities. It may be studying for something or simply getting to work earlier. I have found that starting my day with a devotional, praying, and writing in my journal sets the tone for my day. It gives me clarity, focus, and allows me to express my gratitude for being alive and for the many blessings in my life.

I do not doubt it will become more difficult to make time for prayer and quiet time as I move forward in my career, get married, and start a family. And yet, because it is a priority, I will continue to make time for it.

I am sharing this because it has been working for me. Many successful people talk about prayer and quiet time in the morning and how beneficial it is as one of their habits. What works for you may look a bit different from what works for me. I encourage you to find out what morning prayer or quiet time looks like for you.

REST

It may seem odd to put rest in the *Consistent Focused Action* Section. Let me explain. Rest is imperative to our survival as humans. When I say rest, I am talking about time to allow your mind and body to recover: sleep, leisure time, and time free of external stimulants. Some people thrive with five hours of sleep, some with five hours and a midday nap. Yet others require much more sleep to operate effectively. Whatever it is for you, be consistent with that amount of sleep.

Rest is not synonymous with inaction. You are in fact allowing your body to take the time it needs to take action: to heal, to process, and to reenergize itself. To recover. And in many instances, allowing your mind to organize itself and refocus.

IMPORTANT: If all you do is "rest", you are being lazy, and you may want to reevaluate your approach to life. Let me restate: You should reevaluate your life, your priorities, and how you are stewarding the time and talents you have.

Similar to discovering your own abilities and passions, I cannot tell you how you should rest, but I can share some methods I use. Even up to last year, I felt that "rest was for the weak", and that if I was resting then I was not working and thus wasting time. From discussions with people I admired for consistently getting the right things done, I realized all action is not equal.

Enduring Urgency is a long-term strategy, a lifestyle which accounts for the need for rest as part of the consistent focused action which is required to live effectively.

In college, I recognized my effectiveness sweet spot was working until 11 pm, then waking up at 5:30 am to finish whatever homework I still had. Initially, I was frustrated that I could not stay awake until 2am like some of my friends (this was me suffering from comparison). In time, I became aware that my brain was fresh and recharged when I awoke so I was often able to accomplish the remainder of the work in substantially less time than if I had tried pushing until 2am.

Now, I have gotten used to falling asleep around 10:30 pm and waking up at 4:30am to study, read, or write in my journal. This is part of knowing yourself and adapting to your needs in order to maximize your effectiveness.

In time, my sleep needs may change again, and I will adjust my schedule to enable me to operate effectively.

Urgency vs. Hurriedness

We must take a moment to differentiate between urgency and hurriedness. The difference can be found in their definitions.

Hurried: going or working at speed; done in a hurry; haste[28]

Urgency: Importance requiring swift action

The word hurried is not bad, it is simply incomplete for the stakes at which Enduring Urgency is required. The definition of urgency identifies the uniqueness of this idea. *Importance requiring swift action.* There is something pressing; action that must be taken, and must be taken now because of the importance of the situation. Hurriedness speaks to possibly being out of control. Urgency speaks to being deliberate and taking focused action.

TRAVEL

Here's another idea that may seem out of place. Whenever you are able, travel. If you cannot travel to another country, travel to another state. If you cannot travel to another state, travel to another city. If you cannot travel to another city, travel to another community within your own city.

"Perhaps travel cannot prevent bigotry, but by demonstrating that all peoples cry, laugh, eat, worry, and die, it can introduce the idea that if we try and understand each other, we may even become friends." –

Maya Angelou[29]

We do not see the world as it is, we see the world as we are. And because of this, travel expands our perspective and increases our awareness. Traveling breaks preconceived ideas and expands our understanding of people and of ourselves. It can change our perspective if we begin with an open mind.

Over the past five years, I have been blessed to travel to many countries across Africa and Asia, and states across the USA. In truth, many of the people I have interacted with are dealing with similar life issues, are passionate about their communities, and want to improve them. Some are using what they have to do good where they are. Others are figuring out how they can make an impact. And yes, there are some who are struggling to survive. The same can be said of each of the communities I have lived in throughout my life in Texas, California, Washington D.C., Japan, and New Jersey.

Just as learning another language gives you insight and empathy for people who speak your primary language as their second (or third), traveling gives you insight and empathy for people visiting your country.

As you travel, you are able to see places and experience people for yourself rather than relying solely on what you have heard from other people or read in books. When you travel, interact with the people who live there. In time you will learn they are not so different from you.

CROSS-COMMUNITY COLLABORATION

Collaboration (noun): to work jointly with others or together especially in an intellectual endeavor[30]

"Iron sharpens iron." One aspect of consistent focused action that I wanted to be sure to include is the idea of collaboration. This word has been on my mind and in my heart for the past five years. But its importance to me originates further back.

My first experience with collaboration happened at an early age. My biological mom Genevieve passed away from breast cancer when I was three. My sister was six, my brother was ten. My dad was 36 at the time of my mom's death. My dad was suddenly solely responsible for the health, well-being, and success of three rambunctious children. Fast-forward 25 years, and my older brother is a software engineer, my sister is a family law attorney, and I am a civil engineer turned businessman. More than that, my two older siblings are caring, funny, intelligent, and all-around good people. And I'd like to think I am as well. So, what were the external factors that enabled us to be where we are today? I believe there were several factors: God, my dad, my biological mom Genevieve, my mom Bunmi, and the collaboration that stemmed from our church and family friends in the early years.

It is experiencing the fifth factor that I believe has shaped my world-view and has laid the foundation for Delivering Ideas that Change Everything, Inc and The DICE Initiative. At the heart of my desire to establish DICE is an extreme gratitude to the family and friends who collaboratively raised us and who supported our family during dark days and long nights. This does not discount the incredible work that my dad did in raising us on his own for 10 years, he is my hero. Nor does it discount the impact that my mom, Bunmi, has had in the last 15 years. It simply acknowledges that collaboration maximized our potential for success.

The saying, "It takes a village to raise a child" is true. And at the core of that saying is collaboration – a group of people passionate about the success of a child, committed to working together to maximize the potential for success for that child. It took collaboration to raise us three older Brown-Dawson children, as it is taking collaboration to raise the youngest member of our Brown-Dawson bunch.

DICE is centered around this idea of Cross-Community Collaboration. It is a team and a platform for young leaders to come together, build relationships with other young leaders in our communities and other communities, and collaborate on passion projects to improve our communities. It takes a village to raise a child. And it takes collaboration to improve a community. DICE is Cross-Community Collaboration. The world is our community. And my hope is that we leave behind this notion of success being a zero-sum game, and work together as one to maximize the good we can do within and across our communities.

Dr. Martin Luther King, Jr once said, "Life's most persistent and urgent question is: what are you doing for others?" This is our answer. This is our team. This is our platform. This is The DICE Initiative.

What are you doing for others? What can you do for others today?

Life's most persistent
and urgent question is:
What are you doing for others?
-Dr. Martin Luther King, Jr.

I DARE YOU!

Here it is. The Enduring Urgency strategy laid out for you. Now you have a choice to make. You can choose to close this book and put it back on the shelf or table, and not implement the strategy. Or you can keep this book with you, refer to it often, and use it to improve your life.

I truly believe that if each person lived with Enduring Urgency, if each person stewarded their ideas, talents, and time in service of that important thing to them, the world would not lack. It is those who have chosen to live a passive, complacent, or apathetic life that have robbed the world of a solution – their product, service, discovery, and creation.

I DARE YOU to reflect on your life up to this point and acknowledge whether or not you are living with Enduring Urgency – an understanding that you do not have forever on this earth, so you embrace life, do good, and create a legacy that will last long after you're gone.

I DARE YOU to implement the Enduring Urgency strategy detailed in this book into your daily life.

I DARE YOU to use this book to improve yourself. It will take honest reflection, a willingness to make changes, and action.

I DARE YOU to develop yourself, follow through on your plans, complete your projects, share your thoughts, pursue your passions, and walk in your purpose.

I DARE YOU to watch for people in your life and in leadership positions who operate with an enduring sense of urgency.

I DARE YOU to share this book and the strategy of Enduring Urgency with someone who you think may benefit from the words you have read.

Make it a great life, or not. The choice is yours.

<u>What did you get out of this book? Is it what you expected (what you wrote in the introduction)?</u>

ENDURING URGENCY AND THOSE WHO HAVE IT

I believe we can learn from everyone we interact with: we can learn and implement the qualities of people we admire, and we can understand and work to avoid the ineffective or negative attributes from others. Below, I highlight people whom I admire for living with Enduring Urgency. As you will see, the Enduring Urgency mindset can be applied to all professions and communities. This is list is ever-growing and I have only included a few of the many I could have chosen.

Akon (@akon) is a Senegalese-American entrepreneur, singer, record producer, philanthropist who is currently building a solar-powered city complete with its own cryptocurrency in Senegal. He understands the enduring urgency mindset and is operating with that mindset.

Shaun King (@shaunking) is a writer, activist, and educator who has been through more than his fair share of adversity. Despite or perhaps because of his experiences, he lives with an enduring sense of urgency, and is working to improve the country.

Dwayne "The Rock" Johnson (@therock) is a wrestler and football player turned acting superstar. His story of going from having seven US dollars to his name, to becoming a millionaire movie star and household name is a perfect story of someone operating with Enduring Urgency.

Angela Rye (@angelarye) is an attorney and the CEO of Impact Strategies, a political advocacy firm in Washington, D.C. Her dedication to building up her community is both needed and encouraging. Her "work woke" campaign added the consistent focused action to the knowledge, awareness, and self-love that was captured by "stay woke".

Tobe Nwigwe (@tobenwigwe) is a lyricist who creates uplifting music and music videos encouraging people to live purposeful lives. I first came across his Instagram page when he had a few thousand followers. I watched as he consistently delivered a video weekly with him freestyling and his wife and friends dancing alongside him. Listening to the lyrics and watching the video creations was great and seeing him reach 100,000 followers a couple months later was justified.

Nipsey Hussle was musician, businessman, community activist from Los Angeles who constantly put gems of wisdom into his lyrics to uplift, educate, and empower his community. His message of life being a marathon is congruent with the Enduring Urgency mindset. His death on March 31, 2019 (my 28th birthday) reminds me to live with Enduring Urgency.

I will list others for you to look up in your leisure: Maxine Waters, Dr. Eric Thomas, Gary Vaynerchuk, Elon Musk, Jessica Lashawn, Stephen Furtick, Dr. Dharius Daniels, Michael Broussard, Robert F. Smith, John Lewis, T.D. Jakes.

SOME BOOKS I'VE READ:

As I have stated before, the thoughts contained within are a combination of the people I have met, the lessons I have learned, and the books I have read throughout the course of my life. Here are some of the ones that made the biggest impact.

The Alchemist by Paulo Coelho

The Memo: Five Rules for Your Economic Liberation by John Hope Bryant

The Circle Maker by Chris Batterson

SOAR by T.D. Jakes

Linchpin by Seth Godin

Tribes by Seth Godin

Option B by Sheryl Sandberg and Adam Grant

Originals by Adam Grant

The Hate U Give by Angie Thomas

Secrets of Ancient Chinese Art of Motivation by Ong Hean-Tatt

A Wrinkle in Time by Madeleine L'Engle

Ender's Game by Orson Scott Card

The Color of Law by Richard Rothstein

Give and Take by Adam Grant

David and Goliath by Malcolm Gladwell

The Tipping Point by Malcolm Gladwell

Without Their Permission by Alexis Ohanian

The Emotionally Healthy Leader by Peter Scazzero

The Compound Effect by Darren Hardy

I Dare You! By William H. Danforth

Post Traumatic Slave Syndrome by Dr. Joy DeGruy

Ghost Fleet by August Cole and P. W. Singer

The Speed of Sound by Eric Bernt

RePresent Jesus by Dr. Dharius Daniels

Leaders Eat Last by Simon Sinek

Together is Better by Simon Sinek

Rework by Jason Fried and David Heinemeier Hansson

SCRUM: The Art of Doing the Work in Half the Time by Jeff Sutherland

Between the World and Me by Ta-Nehisi Coates

Love Does by Bob Goff

The Secret by Rhonda Byrne

Fight by Craig Groeschel

Oneness Embraced by Dr. Tony Evans

Homegoing by Yaa Gyasi

Dreams from My Father by Barack Obama

The Martian by Andy Weir.

The Bible

THANK YOU

I would like to thank my family and close friends, who have encouraged me, supported me, and kept me humble throughout my life. I know I would not be the man I am today without each of you.

There's a saying that you are the average of the five people you spend the most time with. Though I have spent no time with any of them one-on-one, their messages and words pour into me and each of their spirits found its way into the pages of this work. One of those people is Dr. Dharius Daniels and another is Pastor Stephen Furtick. The third is Bishop T.D. Jakes. The other two over the past couple years are Nipsey Hussle and J. Cole. Thank you, gentlemen, for your truth, wisdom, and empowerment.

A special Thank You to Merrick. In April of 2018, she wrote me a message that said, "You should write a book on resiliency! I like hearing your insights."

Since then, I have researched and thought a lot on the topic of resilience – what it is, how it is developed, and why it is needed now. Her message was the fertilizer to grow the seeds into this book. Her words gave me a sense of urgency as I thought of someone waiting to read my book whose life would be changed by the words within. Thank you, Merrick, for providing the encouragement and urgency for this project.

Notes

[1] The West Wing, Season 2 Episode 10

[2] "Urgency: Definition of Urgency by Lexico." Lexico Dictionaries | English, Lexico Dictionaries, www.lexico.com/en/definition/urgency (accessed May 21, 2018).

[3] Honi the Circle Maker – Schram, Peninnah. "Spirit of Trees." Spirit of Trees, Spirit of Trees, 6 May 2012, spiritoftrees.org/honi-and-the-carob-tree (accessed July 15, 2018).

[4] "Resilience: Definition of Resilience by Lexico." Lexico Dictionaries | English, Lexico Dictionaries, www.lexico.com/en/definition/resilience (accessed May 21, 2018).

[5] Reivich, Karen J., et al. "Master Resilience Training in the U.S. Army." American Psychologist, vol. 66, no. 1, 2011, pp. 25–34., doi:10.1037/a0021897.

[6] "Resilience." Merriam-Webster, Merriam-Webster, www.merriam-webster.com/dictionary/resilience (accessed May 21, 2018).

[7] "Adversity." Merriam-Webster, Merriam-Webster, www.merriam-webster.com/dictionary/adversity (accessed May 21, 2018).

[8] DuVernay, Ava, director. A Wrinkle in Time. A Wrinkle in Time, Walt Disney Pictures, 2018.

[9] "Search Results for 'Charles+Swindoll+Life+Is+10' (Showing 1-0 of 0 Quotes)." Goodreads, Goodreads, www.goodreads.com/search?q=charles%2Bswindoll%2Blife%2Bis%2B10&search%5Bsource%5D=goodreads&search_type=quotes&tab=quotes (accessed July 15, 2018).

[10] Grover, Tim S. "It's Not Selfish to Focus on Yourself. The More You Improve, the Better You Can Take Care of All Those Important People You're Grateful for Today." Twitter, Twitter, 23 Nov. 2017, twitter.com/attackathletics/status/933794009109204993.

[11] Daniels, Dharius. Represent Jesus: Rethink Your Version of Christianity and Become More like Christ. Charisma House, 2014.

[12] "A Quote by Michael Jordan." Goodreads, Goodreads, www.goodreads.com/quotes/569703-i-have-failed-many-times-and-that-s-why-i-am (accessed July 15, 2018).

13 "Search Results for 'James+Stockdale+Confront+the+Brutal+Facts' (Showing 1-0 of 0 Quotes)." Goodreads, Goodreads, www.goodreads.com/search?utf8=%E2%9C%93&q=james%2Bst ockdale%2Bconfront%2Bthe%2Bbrutal%2Bfacts&search_type=q uotes.

14 "Patience: Definition of Patience by Lexico." Lexico Dictionaries | English, Lexico Dictionaries, www.lexico.com/en/definition/patience (accessed May 21, 2018).

15 "Complacency: Definition of Complacency by Lexico." Lexico Dictionaries | English, Lexico Dictionaries, www.lexico.com/en/definition/complacency (accessed January 24, 2020).

16 Used with permission from Dr. Dharius Daniels. "Don't Sleep", Lead Pastor of Change Church.

17 McConaughey, Matthew. "Acceptance Speech - Who I Chase." YouTube, YouTube, 2014, www.youtube.com/watch?v=wD2cVhC-63I (accessed January 24, 2020).

18 "A Quote by Nelson Mandela." Goodreads, Goodreads, www.goodreads.com/quotes/16243-education-is-the-most-powerful-weapon-which-you-can-use (accessed January 24, 2020).

19 "Action: Definition of Action by Lexico." Lexico Dictionaries | English, Lexico Dictionaries, www.lexico.com/en/definition/action (accessed May 21, 2018).

20 "Focused Adjective - Definition, Pictures, Pronunciation and Usage Notes: Oxford Advanced American Dictionary at OxfordLearnersDictionaries.com." Focused Adjective - Definition, Pictures, Pronunciation and Usage Notes | Oxford Advanced American Dictionary at OxfordLearnersDictionaries.com, www.oxfordlearnersdictionaries.com/us/definition/american_english /focused (accessed January 24, 2020).

21 "Consistent." Merriam-Webster, Merriam-Webster, www.merriam-webster.com/dictionary/consistent (accessed January 24, 2020).

22 Nightingale, Earl. "The Strangest Secret." YouTube, YouTube, www.youtube.com/watch?v=EFhkdzj-x80.

23 "Chapter 5." I Dare You!, by William H. Danforth, American Youth Found, 1983, pp. 116–116.

[24] "Chapter 5." I Dare You!, by William H. Danforth, American Youth Found, 1983, pp. 88–88.

[25] "Consistency." Merriam-Webster, Merriam-Webster, www.merriam-webster.com/dictionary/consistency (accessed January 24, 2020).

[26] "Consistency." Merriam-Webster, Merriam-Webster, www.merriam-webster.com/dictionary/consistency (accessed January 24, 2020).

[27] "Distraction." Merriam-Webster, Merriam-Webster, www.merriam-webster.com/dictionary/distraction#other-words (accessed January 24, 2020).

[28] "Hurried." Merriam-Webster, Merriam-Webster, www.merriam-webster.com/dictionary/hurried (accessed January 24, 2020).

[29] Angelou, Maya. "A Quote from Maya Angelou." Goodreads, Goodreads, www.goodreads.com/quotes/546179-perhaps-travel-cannot-prevent-bigotry-but-by-demonstrating-that-all (accessed January 24, 2020).

[30] "Collaboration." Merriam-Webster, Merriam-Webster, www.merriam-webster.com/dictionary/collaboration (accessed January 24, 2020).